The American Darts
Organization
Book of Darts

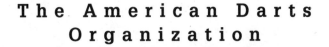

The American Darts
Organization

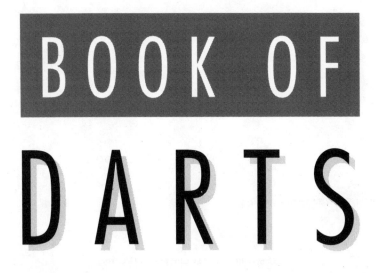

BOOK OF

DARTS

Chris Carey

L&B

Lyons & Burford, Publishers

Printed in the United States of America

Design by Richard Oriolo

Illustrations by Manuel F. Cheo

10 9 8 7

Library of Congress Cataloging-in-Publication Data

Carey, Chris.
    The American Darts Organization book of darts / Chris
Carey.
        p.   cm.
    Includes index.
    ISBN 1-55821-247-7
    1. Darts (Game) I. American Darts Organization. II.
    Title. III. Title: Book of darts.
GV1565.C37   1993
794.3—dc20   93-37443
                                                        CIP

With special gratitude to my brother, John Carey, who introduced me to darts over a decade ago. And to my wonderful wife, Joanne, who saw how taken I was by the game and kindly bought me my first set of darts shortly thereafter. As she knows, I've been playing as often as I can ever since.

C O N T E N T S

GETTING STARTED

GAMES

Foreword

Darts—to some it's a game, to others it's a sport, and to a select few, it's a profession. The American Darts Organization exists to promote the game of darts for everyone, beginner and professional alike.

I first picked up a dart in late 1968. Before I knew it, I was hooked on the game, involved in running my local league, and serving as a darts consultant for General Sportcraft/Unicorn/Nodor. I began travelling to the few major tournaments in existence at the time and became acquainted with players throughout the United States and Great Britain.

It soon became obvious that our sport needed a national organizing body, similar to those in other countries. With considerable assistance from fellow darter Ed McDevitt (Philadelphia's "Irish Hot Dog"), I proposed the formation of the American Darts Organization (ADO). Together we planned a meeting of darts organizers in conjunction with the Michigan Open tournament in October 1975. With 10-cent beers in hand, Ed and I sat over a pool table and drafted the original bylaws, which were adopted by a majority of the 28 individuals in attendance at the inaugural ADO meeting.

The ADO was chartered in 1976, with 30 local member clubs representing approximately 7,500 players. Today, over 300 associations (some 75,000 players based in all 50 states) are affiliated with the American Darts Organization. This phenomenal growth can be attributed to a variety of factors, not the least of which is the fun and fellowship associated with darts—known around the globe as "the sport that begins and ends with a handshake." In comparison to those of other sports, the basic rules of darts are simple. Darts is relatively inexpensive and requires only a limited amount of court space and no special uniform. Few officials are needed, as the darts "speak for themselves." Participation involves few limitations or prerequisites—age, sex, physical strength, and size have little effect on one's ability to excel.

The existence of the ADO as the national "umbrella" organizing body has contributed greatly to the continued growth of darts in the United States. Over the years, hundreds of individuals have volunteered their time and talents to standardize playing rules, organize local league and tournament activities, obtain sponsorship funding and media recognition, and, in so doing, attract thousands of new players to the game. Thanks to their efforts, $15 million in total prize money has been awarded in 2,500 ADO-sanctioned tournament events since 1975. Men's and Women's National Championships have been established as well as a grassroots playoff program to determine international player/team representation, a National Youth Championship, and a Memorial Scholarship Fund. A U.S. Professional Championship is also in the planning stages.

There is a bright future for the sport of darts in the United States. Increasing participation and nationwide enthusiasm will command media attention, resulting in television exposure and corporate funding. Professional players, whose numbers are growing annually, will help darts gain the recognition it so richly deserves. Their attire, demeanor, and personality appeal are key factors in achieving this goal. Our real future rests with the average league players, however. It is their zest for the game that has attracted, and will continue to attract, new players of all ages to our sport.

We are confident that the publication of *The American Darts Organization Book of Darts* will entice more participation and attract new members to our organization. We are proud to lend our name to a most useful and easily understood book for beginning players.

Chris Carey shares our primary, simple, yet ambitious goal: to promote darts today, thereby assuring continued growth and popularity for our sport in the years ahead.

—Tom Fleetwood
Executive Director
American Darts Organization

Preface

A few years ago, being curious about what was available on this great game I enjoyed playing so much, I began looking for a good book on darts. I quickly discovered that there were very few books, and those that I found were often out-of-date, British in perspective, or entirely too complicated in their approach to introduce the game to a broad audience, including beginners. I figured there had to be an alternative, and this is it: a simple, inexpensive book whose sole aim is to inform everyone, especially beginners, about the basics of the game—from throwing the first dart to the rules and strategies of the most popular games played today.

To begin playing darts, all one needs is the desire to play and basic eye-hand coordination. Readers of *The American Darts Organization Book of Darts* require no previous knowledge or aptitude, and the material is presented in an order that any player should find most useful. Taking it from there and teaching yourself—making the game *yours*—is up to you. If this book helps anyone establish that initial foundation and familiarity with the game, then I have succeeded and the sport of darts has gained another player. Welcome.

No book ever makes it into print without the help of many. Tom and Della Fleetwood of the American Darts Organization have been most generous with their time and encyclopedic knowledge of the game; it's an honor to have their support and to have the name of the American Darts Organization associated with this book. A great debt is owed to Nick Lyons and Peter Burford for their encouragement at every step of the writing and publishing process. Heartfelt thanks are also due to the many friends I have made playing darts; I've learned so much from them, been encouraged and humbled by them, and, most important, had lots of fun.

Getting Started

ONE

A Brief History of Darts

A gaudy dress and gentle air
May slightly touch the heart;
But it's innocence and modesty
That polishes the dart.

—Robert Burns (1759–1796), "Handsome Nell"

Of the history of darts not a great deal is known for certain. It is commonly assumed that the game of darts was a logical outgrowth of archery, and arrows were often called darts, as in the above verse by eighteenth-century Scottish poet Robert Burns (in which the "dart" is Cupid's arrow). Today the opposite is true, for it is quite common to hear "arrows" used as slang for darts.

The game of darts, in its basic form, was born as a sporting game in the English public houses—pubs—

hundreds of years ago. The first darts resembled short, hand-held arrows, and the first dartboards were cross sections of trees or the bottoms of beer barrels. From these early, improvised dartboards the configurations of the modern dartboard were created: The concentric circles and spider pattern of wires of the modern dartboard resemble the cracked, weathered cross sections of trees; the bottoms of beer barrels afforded the perfect bull's-eye—the cork. Today the bull's-eye is still called the "cork."

The history of the game as we know it today in the United States is relatively short. Although there are reports that the game of darts arrived in the New World with the *Mayflower*—and indeed, those early settlers did play a variation of the game called "buttes," using small hand-thrown arrows—the history of darts in America really begins sometime in the late nineteenth century, when immigrants from England brought the game to America. For decades, though, the game was known only in the pubs that were frequented by these immigrants. Because of its national origin, the term "English darts" is still used by many when referring to the modern game using the board, equipment, and games outlined in this book.

In England, during the early decades of the twentieth century, the popularity of darts grew steadily as a sporting pastime in the pubs. In fact, in 1908, darts was officially elevated to a game of skill when a pub owner in Leeds, England, was called before the city magistrates for allowing an illegal "game of chance" to be played in his establishment. As legend has it, the proprietor went to court, with dartboard and darts in hand, and proceeded to throw three darts at a designated numbered segment of the board. He then challenged an officer of the court to match his throw. Not surprisingly, the court clerk could not match the accurate throw, and the judge immediately dismissed the case, since the game of darts was obviously not a game of chance at all, but a *game of skill.*

Gradually this game of skill gathered greater numbers of enthusiastic players in England. More and more pubs put up dartboards and, naturally, local organizations and leagues developed. The first of many national organizations, the National Darts Association, was formed in England in 1924 to sponsor tournaments. In 1927, *The News of the World* newspaper began sponsoring local competitions in London; these later grew into regional and national tournaments. By 1939, the game was so popular that it even entered the tense, wartime political arena. In the interest of domestic stability, it is said that Scottish magistrates decided to ban the game in pubs on the questionable assumption that it fostered bad habits and "ne'er-do-wellism" among the working classes. The public outcry was loud, and the ban never took effect.

In the years since World War II, darts has enjoyed tremendous international growth. Of great importance to this postwar boom were the enormously popular *News of the World* tournaments, which were held annually in England from 1947 to 1990. Through the 1950s and 1960s, local and national tournaments in Great Britain continued to reach larger audiences; in America and elsewhere, the game grew steadily. By the mid-1970s, darts had become so popular in Great Britain

that tournaments were first televised to a wide and ap-
preciative audience.

With this increased visibility of the game as played
by professionals and growing amateur enthusiasm,
darts took off. National and international tournaments
attracted more players and larger prize monies. Almost
simultaneously, major national organizations were
formed to govern these tournaments, attract greater
sponsorship, and promote the sport. The British Darts
Organisation was founded in 1973, the American Darts
Organization in 1975, the National Darts Federation of
Canada in 1977, the Darts Federation of Australia in
1976, and dozens of other national organizations—from
South Africa to Japan to Brazil, and in virtually all the
European countries—were created to help establish
tournaments and promote the sport. Almost all these
national organizations are members of the World Dart
Federation (WDF), founded in 1976, which is recog-
nized as the official governing body for most international competitions.

One of the legendary highlights of darts' recent
growth in popularity was British professional John
Lowe throwing the first televised, perfect nine-dart 501
game in the MFI World Matchplay Championship in
1984. Like pitching a perfect game in baseball, a perfect
501 game is a feat of astounding skill and consistency:
Nine consecutive darts must hit specific target areas on
the dartboard that are about the size of a paper clip. This
historic feat was matched in 1990, again in Great
Britain and on the BBC, when American professional
Paul Lim, representing the American Darts Organization, became the second person to throw a televised, per-

fect nine-dart 501 game in the Embassy World Professional Darts Championship*. John Lowe and Paul Lim are both active on the professional darts scene today.

Since the 1970s the game of darts has spread rapidly across America. There are hundreds of tournaments every year, each offering a surprising amount of prize money. In pubs and restaurants in big cities and small towns alike, there are local leagues and matches, and many of these amateur players aspire to the rapidly growing ranks of professionals. As the general popularity of the game grows and the professional arena swells, sponsorships and tournament prizes are being

---

* For the curious and the envious, here is exactly how these perfect 501 games were thrown, dart by dart (T = triple, D = double; For example, T20 = 60).

John Lowe, October 13, 1984: T20, T20, T20; second turn, T20, T20, T20; third turn, T17, T18, D18 (180 + 180 + 141 = 501).

Paul Lim, January 9, 1990: T20, T20, T20; second turn, T20, T20, T20; third turn, T20, T19, D12 (180 + 180 + 141 = 501).

offered by dart product manufacturers, brewing companies, and other corporations. Today, professionals compete for more than $1 million in prize money annually in the United States alone.

But even with television coverage, more tournaments, greater prize money, growing organizations, and rapid expansion at the local level, the game of darts still owes a great deal to its simple origin in the pubs of England, for therein lies much of the enduring history and the traditions of the game—namely, that darts began, and continues today, as a friendly pub sport.

Equipment

The equipment needed to play darts is straight-forward:

- ➤ A good dartboard, either a bristle board for steel-tip darts or a plastic/nylon board for soft-tip darts (from $35 to $60)
- ➤ Darts, either steel-tip or soft-tip (from $10 to $100 or more for a set of three)
- ➤ *Or* a combination set of darts, dartboard, score-board, cabinet, and other accessories (from $75 to $200)
- ➤ A safe, well-lighted place to play

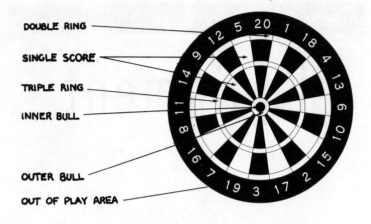

DOUBLE RING

SINGLE SCORE

TRIPLE RING

INNER BULL

OUTER BULL

OUT OF PLAY AREA

Dartboards

The standard international dartboard is known as the "clock" board. It is 18 inches in diameter and has 20 numbered, pie-shaped segments of equal size, plus the bull's-eye. Each numbered segment has a double ring on the outside perimeter of the scoring area and an interior triple ring (which count double and triple of that number, respectively). The bull's-eye has an outer bull area (also known as a single bull's-eye, which scores 25) and an inner bull (also known as a double bull's-eye, which scores 50).

➤ For Steel-Tip Darts ◄

The best dartboards available for steel-tip darts are "bristle" boards, which are made by a number of reputable manufacturers and are available at sporting-goods or dart-supply stores. These dartboards are made from millions of tightly packed, threadlike plant fibers bound by a two-inch steel band, with thin wires attached to delineate the segments of the scoring surface. Less expensive boards made of paper, cork, or other porous, composite materials are available and may be suitable for occasional home use, but bristle boards are standard in all national and international tournaments and local league competitions. A good bristle board will last months—even years—depending on the amount of play, as long as it isn't exposed to extreme heat or moisture.

➤ For Soft-Tip Darts ◄

Over the past few years, soft-tip, or "electronic" darts, as they're commonly called, have become increasingly popular. Today many people are discovering darts for the first time on dartboards attached to electronic, coin-fed scoring machines in taverns and restaurants and their popularity has spawned leagues and tournaments worldwide. The board has the same numbers, configuration, and dimensions as the bristle board, but it is made of durable, hard plastic or nylon, with hundreds of small holes in it. The thin, hard nylon point of the special soft-tip dart sticks in the holes of the board. With electronic boards, the dart tip triggers an electronic response, and the score appears on a lighted display. *Steel-tip darts cannot be used on these boards.*

➤ Choosing the Right Dartboard for You ◄

Just a few years ago, the bristle board was the primary choice, and it is still the favorite of traditionalists and the standard for all major international tournaments. Today, though, with the growing popularity and availability of soft-tip darts, players have a choice. Try to play on both before you make your decision and see which kind you like best. Also, if you're interested in joining a league, you should probably choose the type of board the league plays on.

Setting Up a Dartboard

➤ Height: 5 feet 8 inches from floor to center of bull's-eye.

➤ Distance from *front of board* to throwing line: 7 feet 9¼ inches. To mark the throwing line on the floor, a piece of tape will do. Major tournaments, however, are played with a "hockey" (also spelled "oche"—pronouced *ockey*), which is a thin, raised strip of wood approximately 1½ inches high.

➤ Mounting: Flush to the wall—not leaning like a picture—with the 20 always at the top; the 20 is always a dark section or "pie." Most dartboards come with instructions and a mounting bracket that easily attaches to the wall at the correct height.

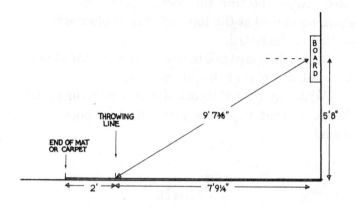

➤ Location: Since darts often bounce out of the board, never put a board up near windows or breakables or where anyone could accidentally walk into the playing area between the throwing line and the dartboard.

➤ Care and Maintenance ◄

A good bristle board needs little care. However, bristle boards should be regularly "rotated" as they get worn from play. The metal or plastic ring surrounding the board that holds the numbers is attached by small brackets and can easily be moved. Since dartboards can wear irregularly (with the highest number, 20, usually receiving the most use), rotating this ring periodically will lengthen the life of the board and make for better darts. After rotating the number ring, the 20 should again be placed at the top and should always be a dark section of the board.

A bristle board not in use should be stored in a box in a cool, dry place to avoid warpage.

With any type of board, if it gets worn or broken to the point that it affects your game, it should be replaced.

Darts

Darts are available in many different sizes, styles, and weights, and the serious dart player may experiment with many different darts before finding the right set. However, *there is no wrong or right type of dart: The right darts are the ones that feel comfortable to the player*, as long as they are within official specifications (maximum weight allowable in tournament play is 50 grams; maximum length is 12 inches). Some very good dart players use inexpensive brass darts and others play with expensive, even custom-made models.

Although some inexpensive darts do not come apart in components, all better darts are made of assembled components so that if they should break (from bouncing out of the board or being hit by other darts), they can be easily repaired. This also allows players to experiment with different parts, particularly flights and shafts.

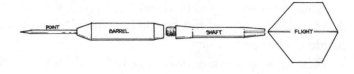

➤ Basic Components of the Standard Dart ◄

➤ **The point and the barrel.** The point is usually made of steel; it is fused to the barrel, which can be made of brass, nickel-silver, or tungsten alloy. With soft-tip darts, the nylon point screws into the barrel and is removable, since it may break or bend and need to be replaced.

➤ **The shaft.** The shaft screws into the barrel and is commonly made of durable plastic or nylon or light metal; they are available in a number of different styles, colors, and lengths.

➤ **The flight.** The flight is the colorful "feathers" of the dart; it fits into pre-cut slots on top of the shaft. They are often made of plastic, nylon, metal, or fabric; actual feathered flights are also available.

➤ Choosing the Right Darts for You ◄

Dart players today have a wide assortment of darts from which to choose: heavy or light, short or long, bulky or thin, with a variety of gripping surfaces and styles of flights and shafts. If you can, experiment with several styles before purchasing a set; if this isn't possible, your first set of darts should simply feel comfortable in your hand and not be too expensive, should you decide to change.

The least expensive darts are made of inexpensive metals, usually brass. Today, thinner, more streamlined darts made of heavier metals, usually a tungsten alloy, are most popular with league and tournament players. These thinner darts are more comfortable to throw for many, and they allow the best players a much tighter grouping without interference from other darts. The most common weights are 14 to 30 grams, but lighter and heavier models are available

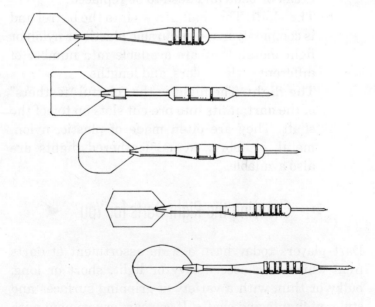

A sampling of the styles and shapes of darts available.

Accessories, Innovations, and Safety

➤ Accessories ◄

Most sporting-goods or dart-supply stores or catalogs offer a variety of accessories. Among the most useful are the following:

➤ **A rubber mat.** A mat is a good idea on hard floors. The standard mat is about 30 inches wide and about 10 feet long, with the throwing line clearly marked.

➤ **A cabinet or backboard.** Some sort of backboard should be placed behind the dartboard to protect the wall—either by mounting the board in a dartboard cabinet or by placing some protective cover behind the board. Most stores that sell dart supplies carry sturdy fabric-covered backboards, but there are also do-it-yourself options, including a three-foot-square remnant of carpet, or a piece of soft wood or thick, corrugated cardboard. Most cabinets have scoreboards on the doors, and some come with built-in lights.

➤ **A scoreboard.** A basic blackboard and chalk will do for scoring, but other scoreboards are available that use chalk or erasable pens. Most scoreboards come with the scoring grids for the popular games Cricket and '01 already printed on them.

➤ **Lighting.** Depending on available light, a basic

spotlight that provides bright, shadowless illumination of the dartboard is advisable.

➤ **Other accessories.** Dart-sharpening stones, dart carrying cases, and other less-essential equipment are available wherever darts are sold.

➤ Innovations in Darts and Dartboards ◄

As the number of dart players grows, manufacturers and players are developing new—and often better—styles of darts and innovations in dartboards. Among the more popular are the following:

➤ **Retractable-point darts.** These steel-tip darts, commonly called Hammer Heads, Power Points, and other similar brand names, have points that automatically retract slightly when they hit the dartboard. This makes them less likely to bounce out of the board when they strike a wire, and stick on one side or the other.

➤ **Convertible-tip darts.** Screw-in, steel-tip points are available to convert soft-tip darts for play on bristle boards.

➤ **Other dart innovations.** Recently, manufacturers have been experimenting with different styles, balances, and grips of darts. These innovations include extra-long points, a wide variety of gripping surfaces on the barrel—from simple parallel grooves cut in the metal to rough, etched, knurled surfaces—and a number of weighting variations (e.g., front-weighted, or

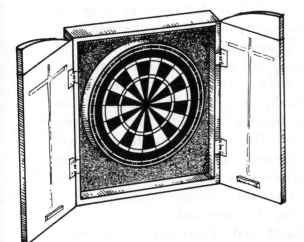

Two options for setting up a dartboard:
in a cabinet or with a backboard.

torpedo-shaped darts that carry more weight toward the point) to accommodate individual throwing techniques. Shafts are available in plastic, metal, and some plastic-and-metal combinations, all in a variety of lengths and styles.

➤ **Professional practice dartboards or "Championship" boards.** These dartboards are for practice only; the triple and double rings are about half the width of those on a standard board.

➤ **Sunken-wire dartboards.** These bristle boards have either beveled or sunken wires to decrease the frequency of bounce-outs.

➤ **Quadro dartboards.** These dartboards have a "quadro" or "quatro" ring midway between the triple ring and the bull's-eye that counts four times the number. Although these boards are used in some special tournaments, they are considered a novelty by many.

➤ **Bristle dartboards of man-made fibers.** The standard bristle board is made of millions of natural plant fibers (from the tropical sisal plant). Manufacturers are currently developing dartboards made of man-made fibers that have similar properties. Although these dartboards are not yet widely available, if they are successful they may be the dartboards of the future.

➤ Safety ◄

Darts of any kind can bounce out of the board, creating a potential safety hazard for anyone standing within striking range. Steel-tip darts frequently bounce out when they strike a wire; soft-tip darts bounce out when the point just misses the hole in the dartboard. With any kind of dart, the following safety guidelines are very important:

➤ Mount the dartboard in a safe, well-lighted, roomy area.

➤ Never try to catch a dart bouncing off the board.

➤ Never play barefoot or wearing sandals, especially with steel-tip darts.

➤ Always pay attention to the game; never throw a dart without first looking to make sure the playing area is clear.

➤ Very young children and darts don't mix. Keep children and pets well behind the throwing line when playing.

WARNING: Darts is an adult game. Children should play only with adult supervision.

THREE

Techniques for Successful Play

Like any sport that calls for specific physical mechanics and careful eye-hand coordination, to maximize dart skills one needs to develop the optimum motion for successful play. Throwing a dart accurately demands attention to the basics:

➤ Holding the dart—the important first element of play
➤ Stance at the line—maintaining balance and comfort
➤ The mechanics of the throw—setup, release, and follow-through

➤ Concentration
➤ A thorough knowledge of the board
➤ Practice, observation, and experimentation

Holding the Dart

To most people, picking up a dart is not a totally new experience; they know how to hold and throw it "naturally." And although that *may* be the best way to hold the dart, it is worthwhile to consider experimenting with different grips. The most common way to hold a dart is between the thumb and two or three fingers, gripping the barrel firmly, but there are myriad variations, all suited to the individual player. *There is no wrong or right way, just the best way.*

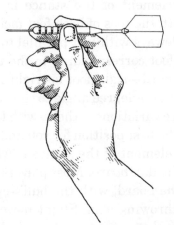

Common way to hold a dart with the thumb and two fingers.

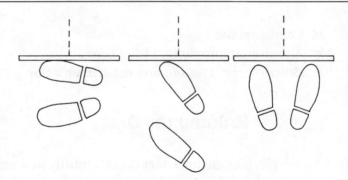

Some typical stances.

Stance

The stance at the throwing line or "hockey" is a critical element of throwing darts accurately. It should complement the *most natural* throwing motion and should offer comfort, stability, and complete balance.

The first element of the stance is foot position. Some stand with the toes of both feet facing the board, some stand sideways with feet parallel to the throwing line (with the foot corresponding to the throwing arm closest to the board—right foot for right-handers), and others stand at a 45-degree angle to the board. Virtually all stances are variations of these, with the feet slightly apart. Find the best position for you and stick to it.

The other element of the stance is where to stand in relation to the dartboard. Most players stand directly in front of the board, with the bull's-eye in a direct line with the throwing arm. Slight movements to the right or left may be necessary when aiming at various numbers or when the line of sight is obscured by another dart in the board. The best players don't move very much between shots, however, and their stance is a never-changing part of their game. After all, that's why they're good: They're consistent and all the parts of their game, physical and mental, work together.

Mechanics of the Throw

The dart throw has three basic steps: stance and setup, release, and follow-through. These integrated motions are similar to the basic elements of the basketball free throw. The fundamental mechanics of a fluid, comfortable, and coordinated motion are the same.

➤ Step One: Stance and Setup ◄

The first step involves assuming the stance, sighting the target (elbow up, upper arm parallel to the floor), and bringing the dart back in front of the face in preparation for the throw. Most players keep the dart directly in front of the face throughout the throwing motion. The elbow remains at approximately the same height during the throw; it is the stationary fulcrum of the entire motion.

➤ Step Two: Release ◄

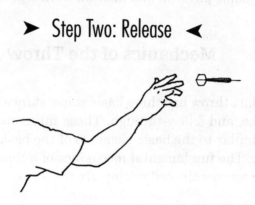

The next step is throwing the dart toward the board, releasing it toward the target. The throwing action is accomplished by a gradual, fluid motion of the forearm as it extends directly toward the dartboard, accompanied by a slight forward movement of the wrist. One of the most common problems for beginning players is not knowing how hard to throw. Accuracy, not force, is the key to successful play, and a dart needs to be thrown only hard enough for it to enter the board—which is only about five feet from the extended arm. The best dart players put a slight, graceful arc in the trajectory of the dart and exhibit a remarkably consistent level of force. Darts are *not* thrown with the full force of the arm or the shoulder.

➤ Step Three: Follow-through ◄

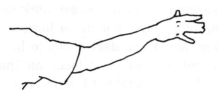

After the dart is released, the arm extends directly toward the dartboard. This may be the most important element for maintaining an accurate and consistent throw. After releasing the dart, the arm follows through naturally (like a tennis serve or a baseball pitch). Throwing darts is *not* a jerky motion. Players should follow the dart into the board both physically and mentally.

➤ Combining Stance with Throwing Motion ◄

The stance at the throwing line and the throwing motion should be natural, comfortable, and effective together. Many potentially good dart players are hampered by lack of balance; as they release the dart, they must lean to keep their balance or raise a foot high off the floor. The best players may raise the rear foot very slightly as they release the dart and shift their weight forward, but they *never* lose their balance.

Concentration

As in other sports, the key to *great* play, assuming that all the basic physical elements are working well, is concentration. Each player has his or her own way of "getting serious" about the dart about to be thrown. The mental discipline needed to focus on the board and tune the rest of the world out is a practiced routine just like the throw itself. And although concentration is hard to discuss and virtually impossible to teach, good players exhibit some common traits related to the inner, mental game:

➤ Total comfort at the throwing line, with attention paid to stance and correct position in relation to the board.

➤ Aiming the dart, physically and *mentally*, and focusing on the dartboard throughout the entire throw.

➤ Throwing the dart consistently, incorporating all the basic elements in concert: setup, release, and follow-through. When this is virtually automatic, players can better concentrate on strategy and scoring.

➤ Treating each and every dart as a new opportunity. Even if the first two darts of a turn miss, the best players remain focused and confident.

➤ Practice and experimentation. Some players even videotape themselves to discover the flaws in their game.

Modeling—Learning from Observation

Beginners, veteran players, and professionals can all learn a great deal from watching others play darts— from the basic mechanics of the stance and throw to the various strategies for winning different games. For beginning and intermediate players, watching others play can be especially rewarding, for they can model their own skills after those more experienced and successful. Or, on the other hand, watching someone who isn't very good—someone always off balance or who throws too hard—can also be a learning experience.

Similarly, partnership play can also often lead to better darts. Being a partner with another player provides a great learning opportunity and frequently produces spirited, confidence-building team competition.

To learn from observation or from playing with others requires careful attention to the basic elements—from stance to follow-through—and diligent practice of new techniques. It is also a good idea to notice other players' decorum and sportsmanship. Darts is a friendly game, no matter how well or how seriously it is played. Every dart game should begin and end with a handshake.

Knowing the Dartboard

To play darts well, you must become completely familiar with all the scoring possibilities and relative dimensions of the dartboard. With regular play, this knowledge comes quickly, and within days or weeks, every beginning player should know where all the numbers are located without looking and know the most common multiple scores (e.g., triple 19 = 57, triple 18 = 54, etc.).

Games

There are many different dart games, and the most popular ones are presented in the following chapters. Some general rules and conventions apply to all these games:

➤ Each turn consists of three darts.

➤ Darts that bounce out or fall out of the board cannot be scored or replayed. In tournament play, there is a five-second rule: A dart must remain in the board for five seconds after the third dart is thrown to count for score.

➤ Darts accidentally dropped can be picked up and thrown.

➤ Usual teams for most games are singles, doubles, or triples (one, two, or three to a team). Opposing team members take alternate turns.

➤ To determine who goes first, players "shoot for cork." Each player (in partnership play, one player from each team) throws one dart for the bull's-eye. The player closest chooses the game to be played, and that team or individual goes first. If it is too close to call, the darts are pulled from the board and thrown again. A double bull's-eye beats a single bull's-eye, and if the first player hits a bull (single or double), the opposing player may ask that the dart be removed before he or she throws to allow for better sighting of the target.

➤ In games with three or more players, playing order may be assigned at random, alphabetically, or by "splashing." To "splash," each player throws *two* darts at the same time and totals the score. These darts are not aimed and are sometimes thrown with the opposite arm (e.g., left-handed for right-handed players) to achieve random results. Both darts must hit the scoring area of the dartboard or must be splashed again. Order of play is determined by high-to-low order of point totals.

➤ In ending a game, all three darts of the turn do not have to be thrown (unless expressly stated in the rules of the particular game).

➤ No part of the foot should extend beyond a clearly marked throwing line.

➤ To ensure accuracy in scoring, the score for a turn should always be recorded *before* the darts are removed from the board.

➤ The player always removes his or her own darts from the board.

➤ If a nonplayer is keeping score, he or she should be quiet, still, and impartial, and should verify each score before the darts are pulled from the board by the player.

➤ A player may approach the board at any time to verify the location of a dart, but no one may touch any dart until the entire turn is completed.

➤ No one should be within two feet of the player throwing—out of consideration and for safety.

➤ Darts is a polite game. Generally, players introduce themselves and shake hands before every game, and a handshake of congratulations after each game is the norm.

➤ For additional detailed rules for tournament play, see Appendix D.

Cricket

Cricket is the most popular dart game played in pubs and game rooms in America today, and it is also a standard tournament game at the local, regional, and national levels. The game is often called Mickey Mouse in England, and it also closely resembles the English game of Chase.

A basic game of accurate and strategic throwing, Cricket is played by everyone. It is easy to learn, but difficult to master. To international players, it may be referred to as American Cricket, since there is a British game of Cricket that is substantially different (see Chapter 14).

NUMBER OF PLAYERS:
Two individual players or two teams.

NUMBERS IN PLAY:
20, 19, 18, 17, 16, 15, and bull's-eye.

RULES OF THE GAME:
The object of Cricket is for each player to hit three of each number—20 through 15—plus three bull's-eyes. The target numbers may be shot in any order but are almost always played in descending order. The first person to "close" all the numbers and the bull's-eye, and to be even or ahead on points, wins. A player "closes" a specific number or the bull's-eye by hitting three of it. The first player to close a number "owns" that number and can score points on it until the competition also

closes it. For example, if one begins a game with four 20s, three "close" the number, plus an additional twenty points are noted on the scoreboard, since the opponent does not have three 20s yet. No points can be scored on a number once both players have closed it.

STRATEGIES FOR SUCCESSFUL PLAY:

Playing a good game of Cricket virtually demands aiming at the triple ring of the target number. Since three of each number are needed, a triple is most valuable and a player can achieve all three with one accurate dart. A perfect opening round in a game would therefore be a triple 20, triple 19, and triple 18. A perfect game could be as short as eight darts: six triples (20, 19, 18, 17, 16, 15) and two darts for bull's-eye (hitting either two doubles or a single and a double). Also, for scoring points the triple ring offers the highest score.

Every Cricket game has two important elements. The first element is rather simple: To win, the player must close all the target numbers. This can be a game in and of itself, called Cricket Without Points. The second element of Cricket, scoring points, is more complicated: The winner must also be tied or ahead in point total. Scoring points in Cricket is a strategic game within a game, since players can score points only on the numbers that they have closed but the opponent has not (scoring on any number ceases once both players have closed it). This important game of points makes Cricket much more interesting and often requires careful strategy decisions with each dart. In short, players may have to decide whether to aim for the numbers that must be closed or to throw for points.

Within many three-dart turns, both options are necessary, and players must decide which to attempt first—points or closing numbers. With the element of points, Cricket becomes a fascinating cat-and-mouse game of offense and defense, as each player tries to close the necessary numbers, score points, and make the right strategy decisions (followed, one hopes, by accurate darts).

Every Cricket game is different, and requires different tactics, but the following general tips outline the fundamentals on which to base a simple, conservative strategy:

➤ Throwing first can be a considerable advantage.

➤ When behind on points, there are two options. One is to begin the turn by throwing for points, if possible, or to attempt to close a number and then score points. The other is to first close the number or numbers the competition may use to score points. These are judgment calls that depend on the players and the score.

➤ When ahead on points, attempt to close numbers, and particularly those numbers that the competition may already be using to score points. But always maintain a comfortable point margin—one that makes the opponent throw at least one dart for points each turn and delays him or her from concentrating on the numbers.

➤ Do not build up excessive points. Excessive point scoring, known as "point mongering," usually only makes the game longer.

➤ Staying ahead on points toward the end of the

game is critical, for many games end up with one player having to hit more bull's-eyes than the other to win: If the opponent's numbers (20-15) are closed, a player must hit additional bull's-eyes to make up any point difference. The bull's-eye counts for 25 points; the double bull's-eye is 50 points.

Scoring:

The scoreboard looks like this (and is often preprinted on standard dart scoreboards):

20
19
18
17
16
15
B

Standard Cricket scoring marks look like this:

/ = one hit
X = two hits
O = three hits, or "closed."

And point scores are listed to the side of the numbered scoring grid, under the players' initials.

Sample Game:

This is an example of an above-average game played by experienced players who are comfortable with the strategies of the game and their individual skills. It is presented as a guideline to show the various possibilities players face with each turn in Cricket.

First turn
Player A hits three 20s. The 20 is closed.
Player B hits a triple 20 and two 19s. The 20 is closed.

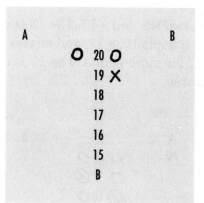

Second turn
Player A hits a 19, a triple 19, and an 18. The 19 is closed and 19 points are scored.
Player B hits a triple 18, misses with another attempt at the 18 for points, and a 19. The 18 and 19 are closed.

Third turn

Player A hits two 18s and a 17. The 18 is closed.
Player B hits a triple 17, a 17, and misses with another
attempt at 17 for more points. The 17 is closed and 17
points are scored.

Fourth turn

Player A hits two 17s and a 16. The 17 is closed.
Player B hits a 16 in three attempts.

```
      A                              B
     /9        O 20 O               /7
               O 19 ⊗
               ∅ 18 O
               ∅ 17 O
               / 16 /
                 15
                  B
```

Fifth turn

Player A hits two 16s and a triple 15. The 16 and 15 are closed.

Player B hits two bull's-eyes, attempting to close the bull's-eye and score points.

```
      A                              B
     /9        O 20 O               /7
               O 19 ⊗
               ∅ 18 O
               ∅ 17 O
               ∅ 16 /
               O 15
                  B ✗
```

Sixth turn

Player A hits one bull's-eye and one 15 (while aiming at the bull's-eye, known as "fallout"). 15 points are scored.

Player B attempts the bull's-eye with all three darts, and hits a double bull's-eye. The bull's-eye is closed and 25 points are scored.

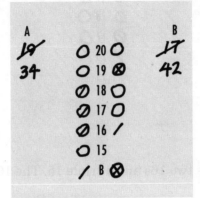

Seventh Turn

Player A hits one bull's-eye in two attempts and one 16. 16 points are scored.

Player B attempts the bull's-eye on all three darts and misses.

Eighth turn
Player A hits one bull's-eye and wins the game.

Variations:

➤ *Cricket Without Points.* The object is to simply hit three of each number, 20-15 and the bull's-eye, in any order. No points are scored.

➤ *Extended Cricket.* A longer game of Cricket—with or without points—in which the numbers 14, 13, 12, 11, and 10 are added to the game. Another version of Extended Cricket includes T for triple and D for double in which one must hit three triples and three doubles (and may also score points on them) in addition to the usual numbers. This game is known as Chase in England and requires careful scoring choices when one hits a triple or a double of a number (a triple 20, for instance, could be scored on the 20, as a required triple on the T, or possibly for points).

➤ *Call Cricket* or *Tactics*. All darts must hit the aimed-for, "called" number; no "fallout"—a common term for unintended, but scorable darts—is allowed. For example, if a player is aiming for the 17 and a 19 is hit, it does not count (toward closing the 19 or for points). To ensure honesty, players frequently announce or "call" the number they are attempting before each throw.

The '01 Games: 301 and 501

Among the first and most popular dart games played everywhere in the world are 301 and 501 (pronounced three-oh-one and five-oh-one). Since the beginning of organized darts, these '01 games, as they're called, have been standard tournament games internationally. The rules and the skills required are deceptively simple.

NUMBER OF PLAYERS:

Any number can play, but usually only two players or two teams.

45

Numbers in Play:

All the numbers are in play, but some receive greater use than others. The 20 and the 19, for instance, are used extensively for scoring points, since they are the highest numbers on the board. All the numbers may be used to throw the necessary doubles in the game.

Rules of the Game:

Each player begins with a score of 301 or 501. The object is to get to zero, exactly, by subtracting each turn score, cumulatively, from 301 or 501.

There are two ways to begin scoring in '01 games: by playing either *double-in* or *straight in*. To double-in one must first hit the double—the outer ring—of any number; that dart score and all subsequent darts count. If no double is hit in a turn, play continues and a double is attempted again in the next turn. When playing straight-in, scoring commences immediately with the very first dart. Generally, 301 is played double-in, and 501 is most frequently played straight-in.

To win any '01 game, the player must hit a double with the last dart to reach the exact score of 0, known as *doubling-out*. For example, with a score of 16 remaining, a player must hit a double 8 to win; with 8 remaining, double 4, and so on. The lowest score allowable in the game is 2 (meaning that double 1 must be thrown to win). Any turn that lowers the score below 2 is void—the player has "busted," and the previous score remains.

Between doubling-in or beginning straight-in to start the game, and doubling-out to end it, the players score as many points as possible per turn and cumulatively subtract the total, beginning with 301 or 501.

STRATEGIES FOR SUCCESSFUL PLAY:

There is no particular strategy in '01. It is a game of accurate, consistent throwing. However, there are three major elements of all '01 games, each requiring specific skills and knowledge: hitting doubles, scoring points, and knowing the scoring possibilities on the board to help tabulate the best "out" to win the game.

A good beginning strategy for doubling-in is to concentrate on either the right or left side of the board, thereby often increasing the likelihood of hitting the desired double or the ones adjacent. By aiming at the 11, for instance, on the left side of the board, one also stands a good chance of "falling out" into the 14 or the 8. The same holds true for the right side of the board with 13, 6, and 10.

Suggested double-in numbers for beginning players.

To score points, players concentrate on the highest numbers on the dartboard, either 20 or 19. The highest score in one three-dart turn is 180: three triple 20s. The common jargon for the highest scores is *a ton* (100 points), *ton-twenty* (120), *ton-forty* (140), and *ton-eighty* (180).

The best strategy for doubling-out is to be comfortable with the following doubles: 20, 16, 12, 8, 4, 2, and 1. But just as important as being able to hit a double to win the game is knowing the best "out." For example, if a player has a score of 154 left, can the game be won in three darts? The answer is yes. The perfect three-dart turn for this would be triple 20 (60 points), triple 18 (54 points), and then, with 40 left, a double 20 to win. The key to ending a game of '01 successfully is to know the outs automatically, quickly recover from missed darts, retabulate the score, and continue.

Many good players are severely handicapped by their unfamiliarity with the board and with the basic mathematics necessary to finish the game. They therefore spend time at the line doing a lot of mental arithmetic or must always depend on an out chart, which tells the player the recommended two- or three-dart "out" for a particular score (see page 52). For example, the highest score one can go out on and win the game is 170. For 170, an out chart would recommend: T20, T20, DB (60 + 60 + game-winning double bull's-eye, 50 = 170).

SCORING:

Scoring in '01 begins immediately when playing straight-in or whenever a double is hit when playing

The most frequently recommended double-out numbers.

double-in. That double and all subsequent darts count in the score to be subtracted from 301 or 501.

To tabulate the score after each turn, it is important to know all the scoring possibilities on the board. This is also a great help as the end of the game approaches.

The scoreboard for '01 notes players' initials at the top and each turn score and remaining game score underneath.

SAMPLE GAME (301 DOUBLE-IN):

First turn

Player A misses on the first dart, then hits a double 16 and a 20. Score: 52.

Player B misses the double ring on all three darts. No score.

Second turn
Player A hits 20, 20, triple 5. Score: 55.
Player B hits a double 11 on the third dart. Score: 22.

Third turn
Player A hits a triple 20, 20, and a 5. Score: 85.
Player B hits three 20s. Score: 60.

Fourth Turn
Player A hits three 20s. Score: 60.
Player B hits a 20, 5, and a 1. Score: 26.

Fifth turn
Player A, with 49 remaining, hits a 9 and a double 20 to win.

	A		B	
	Scored	Remaining	Remaining	Scored
		301	301	
	52	249	279	22
	55	194	219	60
	85	109	193	26
	60	49		

301 Scoreboard at the end of the game.

► How to Read an Out Chart ◄

An out chart is a tabulation of suggested finishes for '01 games. Most players do not follow the out chart all the time, and there are plenty of other game-ending finishes. However, the recommendations of most out charts are based on basic, sensible rules:

> In attempting two- or three-dart outs, the target number for the first dart should never accidentally bust the player. For instance, to finish a game with 52 points remaining, S20, D16 (20 + 32) is a common attempt, but it is not recommended because if the first dart accidentally hit the triple of the 20 (a score of 60), the turn would be over—the player would have busted. For 52 most out charts therefore recommend S12, D20.

> The recommended sequence of two- and three-dart outs usually offers some safety if the last dart is missed. This is why the numbers 20, 16, 12, 8, and 4 are most frequently recommended to finish the game. If the double is missed and a single is hit on these numbers, the player has another opportunity to end the game in one dart. For instance, with 32 points left, a player aims for double 16 but hits a single 16. Now, with 16 left, double 8 can be attempted; if a single 8 is hit instead, leaving 8, double 4 can be attempted, and so on. This is not so, for example, with odd numbers. If one were throwing at double 19 to win and hit a single 19, that would leave 19 points and would require two more darts to win (one option: S3, D8).

Recommended Two- and Three-dart Finishes: Out Chart

T = Triple; D = Double; S = Single; B = Bull's-eye

170 - T20, T20, DB.	127 - T20, T17, D8.	91 - T17, D20.	55 - S15, D20.
167 - T20, T19, DB.	126 - T19, T15, D12.	90 - T18, D18.	54 - S14, D20.
164 - T20, T18, DB.	125 - T18, T13, D16.	89 - T19, D16.	53 - S13, D20.
161 - T20, T17, DB	124 - T20, T16, D8.	88 - T16, D20.	52 - S12, D20.
160 - T20, T20, D20.	123 - T19, T14, D12.	87 - T17, D18.	51 - S11, D20.
158 - T20, T20, D19.	122 - T18, T20, D4.	86 - T18, D16.	50 - S10, D20.
157 - T20, T19, D20.	121 - T17, T18, D8.	85 - T15, D20.	49 - S9, D20.
156 - T20, T20, D18.	120 - T20, S20, D20.	84 - T20, D12.	48 - S8, D20.
155 - T20, T19, D19.	119 - T19, T10, D16.	83 - T17, D16.	47 - S15, D16.
154 - T20, T18, D20.	118 - T20, S18, D20.	82 - T14, D20.	46 - S14, D16.
153 - T20, T19, D18.	117 - T20, S17, D20.	81 - T19, D12.	45 - S13, D16.
152 - T20, T20, D16.	116 - T20, S16, D20.	80 - T20, D10.	44 - S12, D16.
151 - T20, T17, D20.	115 - T19, S18, D20.	79 - T13, D20.	43 - S11, D16.
150 - T20, T18, D18.	114 - T20, S14, D20.	78 - T18, D12.	42 - S10, D16.
149 - T20, T19, D16.	113 - T19, S16, D20.	77 - T15, D16.	41 - S9, D16.
148 - T20, T16, D20.	112 - T20, S12, D20.	76 - T20, D8.	39 - S7, D16.
147 - T20, T17, D18.	111 - T19, S14, D20.	75 - T17, D12.	37 - S5, D16.
146 - T20, T18, D16.	110 - T20, S10, D20.	74 - T14, D16.	35 - S3, D16.
145 - T20, T15, D20.	109 - T20, S9, D20.	73 - T19, D8.	33 - S1, D16.
144 - T20, T20, D12.	108 - T19, S19, D16.	72 - T16, D12.	31 - S7, D12.
143 - T19, T18, D16.	107 - T20, S15, D16.	71 - T13, D16.	29 - S13, D8.
142 - T19, T14, D20.	106 - T20, S14, D16.	70 - T18, D8.	27 - S11, D8.
141 - T20, T19, D12.	105 - T19, S8, D20.	69 - T15, D12.	25 - S9, D8.
140 - T20, T20, D10.	104 - T18, S10, D20.	68 - T20, D4.	23 - S7, D8.
139 - T19, T14, D20.	103 - T17, S12, D20.	67 - T17, D8.	21 - S5, D8.
138 - T20, T18, D12.	102 - T19, S13, D16.	66 - T14, D12.	19 - S3, D8.
137 - T17, T18, D16.	101 - T17, S10, D20.	65 - T11, D16.	17 - S13, D2.
136 - T20, T20, D8.	100 - T20, D20.	64 - T16, D8.	15 - S7, D4.
135 - T20, T17, D12.	99 - T19, S10, D16.	63 - T13, D12.	13 - S5, D4.
134 - T20, T14, D16.	98 - T20, D19.	62 - T10, D16.	11 - S3, D4.
133 - T20, T19, D8.	97 - T19, D20.	61 - T15, D8.	9 - S1, D4.
132 - T20, T16, D12.	96 - T20, D18.	60 - S20, D20.	7 - S3, D2.
131 - T20, T13, D16.	95 - T19, D19.	59 - S19, D20.	5 - S1, D2.
130 - T20, T18, D8.	94 - T18, D20.	58 - S18, D20.	3 - S1, D1.
129 - T19, T16, D12.	93 - T19, D18.	57 - S17, D20.	
128 - T18, T14, D16.	92 - T20, D16.	56 - S16, D20.	

VARIATIONS:

➤ *101.* This short, fast version of '01, played exactly like 301 or 501, can begin double-in or straight-in. A game of 101 can be won in three accurate darts: playing double-in, double 20, triple 15, double 8; playing straight-in, triple 19, 12, double 16. This is a good game for practicing outs under 100.

➤ *401, 501, 601, 701, etc.* The same rules as all other '01 games apply.

➤ *'01 with fast finishes.* Although they are not used in tournament play, there are several unconventional but interesting and challenging fast finishes to '01 games that allow the player to win without throwing a game-winning double. When considering them one must also anticipate the possibility of losing an entire turn of scoring.

   • *111.* With a score of 111, a player may opt to take one dart at the triple 1 to win the game automatically, with the permission of the opponent. If the triple 1 is missed, the turn is over and no score is marked.

   • *222 and 333.* With a score of 222 or 333, a player may opt to throw one dart at triple 2 or triple 3, respectively, to win the game automatically, with the permission of the opponent. If the shot is missed, the turn is over and no score is marked.

   • *Shanghai.* Named after the game of the same name, a *shanghai* is hitting a triple, double, and single of the same number in one three-dart turn. Rarely, this may be used in '01 as a means of winning automatically, providing players agree to its possible use. If the shanghai is missed, the turn is over and no score is marked.

Killer

K iller, as the name suggests, is a spirited, competitive game; it's based on hitting doubles and involves some careful strategy, especially with three or more players.

NUMBER OF PLAYERS:

Any number can play, but Killer is most fun with three or more players.

NUMBERS IN PLAY:

The numbers used are determined by the players. Each player throws one dart with his or her "other" hand (e.g., right-handers throw left-handed) to determine randomly his or her own number. Each player must have a different number. If a player misses the board or hits a number already taken, he or she throws again.

RULES OF THE GAME:

Choosing the order of play with three or more players is arbitrary: by shooting for cork, by "splashing" (see page 32), alphabetically by the players' names, order of lowest-to-highest number each has, or any mutually agreeable order.

Each player first tries to hit the double of his or her *own* number. When this is achieved, the player is known as a "killer," and a K is placed next to his or her initials on the scoreboard. After becoming a killer, a player begins aiming for the doubles of opponents' numbers. Each player has three "lives," and whenever a killer hits an opponent's double, the opponent loses one life. If a killer hits his or her own double by mistake, the killer loses one life; it is therefore possible to kill yourself by accident. It is also possible to kill an opponent in one exceptional three-dart turn by throwing three doubles.

The game progresses until only one person has any lives left.

STRATEGIES FOR SUCCESSFUL PLAY:

Although accuracy is the key to the game, becoming a killer as quickly as possible—preferably first—is often the most important shot in any game of Killer. A player who is accurate on the doubles often wins simply by having more opportunities to throw at opponents' numbers.

Multiple players make Killer a particularly ruthless game, especially when two or more players take aim at the same opponent (known, appropriately, as "ganging up"). The best strategy is to keep careful track of opponents and aim carefully, especially if the doubles in play are adjacent.

Scoring:

Players' initials are listed vertically on the scoreboard in the order of play, with three stripes, or "lives," marked next to them. The players' designated numbers are noted next to their initials. When a player becomes a killer, a K is entered next to his or her initials. Lives are erased as doubles are hit by opponents.

No.	Player	
8	AF	/ / /
17	NL	/ / /
4	PB	/ / /
20	KS	/ / /

Killer scoreboard, noting players' initials, designated numbers, and three stripes—"lives". When a player becomes a killer, a K is marked next to his or her initials.

Variations:

➤ *Killer with Triples.* Played the same way as regular Killer, except that triples are substituted for doubles. Just as regular Killer is great practice for doubles, this variation is solid practice for triples.

➤ *Killer—Straight Off.* After determining the numbers in play, each player begins playing as a killer without having to hit his or her own double first.

➤ *Killer—Don't Hit Your Own!* If a player accidentally hits his or her own double after becoming a killer, the player loses not only one life, but also killer status. The player must hit his or her double again to regain it.

SEVEN

Shanghai

S hanghai is a game of accuracy on the triples and doubles as well as an intense, competitive game of points. A game of "innings," with players always taking an equal number of turns, it is similar to Baseball (see Chapter 8).

NUMBER OF PLAYERS:

Any number can play, and Shanghai is often played with as many as a dozen or more players.

NUMBERS IN PLAY:

1, 2, 3, 4, 5, 6, 7

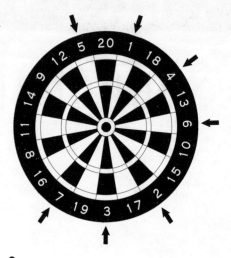

Rules of the Game:

Players take turns throwing at 1, then 2, and so on to 7, in sequence. They try to score as many points as possible, throwing the customary three darts per turn. Only darts hitting the number in play count for score, which is the number value on the board. For example, three 1s count as three points, but three 7s count as 21. So, as the game progresses and the numbers get larger, the fortunes of the game can shift dramatically. There are two ways to win: to get more points than the opponent(s), or to score a shanghai and win automatically. Any player can win automatically in any three-dart turn by hitting the triple, double, and single of the number in play.

Strategies for Successful Play:

The triple is the best area of the number to aim for, as it scores the most points, and it is also the most difficult and necessary target if one is to throw a shanghai and win automatically.

SCORING:

The scoreboard for Shanghai is a simple scoring grid with the players' initials on the top and the numbers 1–7 listed vertically on the left. The cumulative score is marked after each turn so that players can easily keep track of the total score.

SAMPLE GAME:

First inning—1 in play
Player A hits three 1s. Score: 3.
Player B hits a triple 1 and a single 1 (and one dart misses the 1) Score: 4.
Player C hits no 1s. No score.

Second inning—2 in play
Player A hits no 2s. No score.
Player B hits two 2s. Score: 4.
Player C hits a triple and two single 2s. Score: 10

	A	*B*	*C*
1	3	4	-
2	3	8	10
3			
4			
5			
6			
7			

**Shanghai scoreboard after two innings,
noting cumulative scores.**

VARIATIONS:

➤ *Sevens or You're Out.* Sometimes Shanghai is played so that if a specified inning number in rotation is missed completely the player automatically loses. This number is often 3, 5, or the last number in play (usually 7) and is determined before play begins. So, if a player hits no 3s, for example, he or she is out of the game. With three or more players, the other players continue until someone wins.

➤ *Shanghai—Double or Triple Last.* Some variations on throwing a shanghai make it even more difficult to win by hitting a triple, double, and single of an individual number (and that's certainly hard enough) by stipulating that the single cannot be the last dart . Hence, with this rule in force, the triple or double must be the last dart in a turn resulting in a shanghai and winning the game automatically.

➤ *Shanghai—Different Numbers.* Sometimes Shanghai is played with the target numbers chosen at random (instead of 1-7, as noted in rules above). Some play with nine numbers instead of seven (1-9, or others chosen at random).

Baseball

Baseball is an "inning" game of accuracy across a range of numbers, similar to Shanghai. The variation Baseball With Pitching is an excellent game for throwing at the bull's-eye.

NUMBER OF PLAYERS:

Any number can play, but it is usual to have only two players or two teams (like the game of baseball itself).

NUMBERS IN PLAY:

1, 2, 3, 4, 5, 6, 7, 8, 9

Rules of the Game:

Players take turns at the numbers 1 through 9, in sequence—just like the nine innings of a baseball game—and score the number of "runs" hit per "inning." Only darts hitting the number in play count for score, and although double and triple rings count, the numerical value of the number does not. For example, hitting a single of *any* number in play, 1–9, would score only one run (a double, two runs, and a triple, three). A perfect turn or inning would therefore be nine runs (three triples).

The player with the most runs at the end of nine innings wins. In the case of a tie, players may opt to play extra innings and go on to number 10 and beyond, as necessary, with an equal number of turns per player (as in real baseball, with each team having an equal number of times at bat) until someone wins.

Strategies for Successful Play:

The triple is the best area of each number to aim for, as

it affords the highest possible score (three runs) per dart. But one should not try to aim exclusively at the triple ring; aiming for the "fat" part of the number—the single area—and averaging two or more runs per inning will win most games of Baseball.

Scoring:

Like Shanghai, the scoreboard is a scoring grid with the players' initials on the top and the numbers 1 through 9 listed vertically on the left. The score marked after each turn is the cumulative score.

Sample Game:

First inning—1 in play
Player A throws three darts at 1, hits only one. Score: 1.
Player B hits a triple 1. Score: 3.

Second inning—2 in play
Player A hits no 2s. No score.
Player B hits two 2s. Score: 2.

	A	*B*
1	1	3
2	1	5
3		
4		
5		
6		
7		
8		
9		

Baseball scoring after two innings, noting cumulative scores.

VARIATIONS:

➤ *Baseball With Pitching.* This is an excellent game for throwing at the bull's-eye. In the basic game of Baseball, players just "bat" and score runs in each inning of the game. In Baseball With Pitching, players "pitch" as well, which is throwing at the bull's-eye. Each player's turn consists of three darts pitching at the bull's-eye (then pulling them and noting the number of bull's-eyes hit) and then three more darts are thrown (batting) at the inning number, 1–9. The number of runs one gets (from throwing at the designated number) is multiplied by the number of bull's-eyes. For instance, if a player hits two bull's-eyes pitching, the batting score is multiplied by two. If no bull's-eyes are hit, the player may not bat that inning, and 0 is entered for the player's score in that inning. A perfect, and truly exceptional, inning of pitching would be six bull's-eyes—three double bull's-eyes.

SCORING AND SAMPLE GAME OF BASEBALL WITH PITCHING:

The same basic Baseball scoring grid is used.

First inning

Player A hits two bull's-eyes (either two singles or a double bull's-eye), pulls his darts, and then hits two 1s. Score: 4 (number of bull's-eyes times number of runs). Player B hits no bull's-eyes and therefore cannot bat in the first inning. No score.

Second inning
Player A hits no bull's-eyes. No score.
Player B hits three bull's-eyes (either three singles or a double and a single), then hits one 2. Score: 3 (3 bull's-eyes times 1 run).

	A	B
1	4	0
2	4	3
3		
4		
5		
6		
7		
8		
9		

Baseball with Pitching scoreboard after two innings, noting cumulative scores.

Legs

L egs is a simple game in which each player attempts to score the highest number of points in each turn, and must match or or exceed the score of the preceding player. Legs is a great practice game for players who regularly play '01.

NUMBER OF PLAYERS:
Any number can play.

NUMBERS IN PLAY:
All the numbers on the board are used, but players gen-

erally concentrate on the 20 or the 19, since these are the highest numbers on the board.

Rules of the Game:

After determining the order of play, the first player attempts to get the highest score possible and notes it on the scoreboard. The next player must exceed that score, or "lose a leg." Each player starts with three legs and players lose a leg every time they fail to beat the score of the player immediately preceding them. After each turn, players mark the score to beat on the scoreboard. The winner is the last player left with any legs.

Strategies for Successful Play:

Legs calls for accuracy, not strategy, and winning almost always depends on comfort and confidence in aiming for the highest numbers on the board.

Scoring:

Players' initials are listed vertically on the scoreboard in the order of play, with three stripes, or "legs," marked next to them (similar to Killer; see Chapter 6). One stripe is erased each time a player loses a leg.

KS	/ / /
CH	/ / /
DF	/ / /

Legs scoreboard at the beginning of a game,
noting players' initials and three stripes—"legs."

SAMPLE GAME:

Player A hits a double 20, a 1, and one dart misses the board. Score: 41.

Player B hits a 20, a 1, and a 5. Score: 26. Player B loses a leg.

Player A (if only two people are playing) or Player C (if three or more are playing) must then beat a score of 26 or lose a leg.

VARIATIONS:

➤ *Low Legs.* This game has the same general rules, but players attempt to throw the lowest score possible. The preceding score must be beaten by a *lower* score. This variation, like regular Legs, demands accuracy, for the lowest numbers on the board are surrounded by high numbers: 1 is between 20 and 18; 2 is between 17 and 15, and 3 is between 19 and 17.

➤ *Legs—OK to Tie.* Some play that in the case of a tie—when a player matches but does not exceed the score of the previous player—no legs are lost.

➤ *Legs—More than Three Legs.* Although Legs is most frequently played with only three legs per player, it is possible to play a longer game beginning with four, five, or more legs.

TEN

Fifty-One by Fives

Like many dart games, Fifty-One by Fives appears quite simple, but it is difficult to master. Successful play requires considerable accuracy. It's an excellent warm-up or practice game and it is particularly good for practice at 20s and 15s. It is sometimes called All Fives.

NUMBER OF PLAYERS:
Any number can play.

NUMBERS IN PLAY:

All the numbers on the board may be used, but the score of every three-dart turn must be divisible by five, so the most commonly aimed-for numbers are those divisible by five: 20, 15, 10, and 5.

RULES OF THE GAME:

The total points for each turn must be divisible by five to receive any score; the score marked for each turn is determined by the number of "fives" hit. For example, if a player gets 20 points on a turn, the score is 4 (20 ÷ 5 = 4). The last dart of every turn must hit the scoring area of the dartboard or the entire turn is void. Any turn score not divisible by five is not counted. For example, if a player hits a 20, another 20, and then a 1—for a total of 41 points—no score is achieved, since 41 is not divisible by five.

The object of the game is to score exactly fifty-one fives, and *all three darts must score on the last turn.* For instance, with a total score of 47 (47 fives), the next three darts must equal a point total of 20 (or four "fives") to win (47 + 4 = 51). If a player scores too many fives, and is "busted," the turn is over and the score remains the same.

STRATEGIES FOR SUCCESSFUL PLAY:

The best strategy is to know the best scoring possibilities on the dartboard. Two places on the board afford the best opportunities for throwing point totals divisible by five: the 5-20 wedge and the 15-10 wedge. Accuracy in these areas will achieve a high score quickly. Missing these areas means having to throw at other numbers to create a final turn score divisible by five. For more risky play, the bull's-eye and double bull's-eye are also divisible by five (25 and 50 points, respectively), but of course they are considerably harder to hit than the 5, 10, 15, and 20.

Players generally try to avoid reaching scores of 49 or 50 fives. In these cases, since all three darts must be thrown on the last turn, the player must score a total of 10 points with three darts or 5 points with three darts to win. This is much more difficult than it seems. For example, with 49, a player would have to throw a score of 10, for two fives (6, 2, 2 or 7, 2, 1, for example). And attempting to get just one game-winning five with all three darts can be remarkably difficult and frustrating (2, 2, 1 or 1, 1, 3, for example).

Scoring:

Each player simply keeps track of how many fives have been scored and after each turn the cumulative score is marked next to his or her initials on the scoreboard.

Sample Game:

Depending on the player, a game of Fifty-One by Fives can be quick, or as long as 10 or more turns. A perfect game would take only two turns—six darts. Here are a couple of variations on that exceptional game (T = triple; S = single):

1st turn: T20, T20, T20 (180 points = 36 fives)
2nd turn: T20, S10, S5 (75 points = 15 fives)
or
1st turn: T15, T15, T15 (135 points = 27 fives)
2nd turn: T15, T20, T5 (120 points = 24 fives)

Remember: All three darts must be thrown and scorable on the last turn!

Variations:

> *Fifty-Five by Fives.* In this common variation, the same rules apply, but the total number of fives must equal 55. Similarly, for a shorter game, players could play for a lower number.

ELEVEN

Round the World

R ound the World, also known as Round the Clock, is a standard game and is an excellent practice routine for players at any level. Since all the numbers are used, it is also an excellent game for beginners who are just becoming familiar with the dartboard.

NUMBER OF PLAYERS:

Any number can play.

NUMBERS IN PLAY:

All the numbers, 1 through 20, are used (with variations, the bull's-eye is also included).

Rules of the Game:

The object of the game is to hit each number on the board, 1-20, in sequence, once, before the opponent(s). Any part of the number—single, double, or triple—counts. After hitting the number in play, the player may proceed to the next number in rotation. The first to hit all the numbers, in order, wins. Hitting any number out of order does not count. A perfect first turn, for example, would be hitting, in order, 1, 2, and 3.

Strategies for Successful Play:

Accuracy is necessary, but hitting the triple or the double ring is not, so aiming for the "fat" part of the number—the section from the triple ring out to the double ring—is the safest aiming strategy.

Scoring:

Players simply list their initials in order of play on the scoreboard, and after each turn the player notes on the board the next number in play. For example, after a turn ending in hitting the number 3, the number 4 is posted on the scoreboard next to the player's initials.

Variations:

➤ *Round the World With Bull's-eye.* The bull's-eye is added to either the beginning or the end of the game. This can change the game considerably. Requiring the bull's-eye at the end of the game, for example, might allow a player to catch up if the competition can't hit the bull's-eye; similarly, when beginning the game with the bull's-eye, the first to hit it might take a commanding lead if the competition fails on a turn or two. An even more challenging variation is Round the World With Bull's-eye—Beginning and Ending.

➤ *Round the World—Doubles.* This is the same general game, but each player must hit the double of each number, 1-20, in order (with or without including the double bull's-eye). This is great practice for '01 games in which one must double-in and double-out (see Chapter 5).

➤ *Round the World—Triples.* Each player must hit the triple of each number, 1–20, in order. This can be a very long game, even with very good players.

➤ *Round the World—Continuous.* Continuous turns may be taken if a player throws a "perfect turn"—hitting the three numbers in play in order. For example, if a player hits 1, 2, and 3 on the first turn, darts are pulled and the player may take another turn immediately. With these "bonus turns," the turn is over when the player misses a number in rotation, even if only one or two darts have been thrown in that turn. In this variation, a player could win without the opponent(s) ever throwing a dart.

➤ *Round the World With Triples and Doubles.* Hitting triples and doubles of the number in play is rewarded by allowing the player to "skip" the next number or numbers in sequence. If a player hits a triple of the number in play, he or she may immediately proceed two numbers ahead (for example, when throwing at the 1 and a triple 1 is hit, the player may skip the numbers 2 and 3). If a player hits a double of the number in play, the next number in sequence can be skipped. However, players are not allowed to skip the last number in play—usually 20 or bull's-eye.

➤ *Round the World With Triples and Doubles, Continuous.* The two preceding variations are combined, with triples and doubles rewarded by allowing the player to skip numbers, and a perfect turn of hitting the numbers in rotation without missing is rewarded by extra turns.

TWELVE

Halve-It

Halve-It is a game requiring considerable skill. It is among the standard games played by professionals who compete in the the British and American Pentathlon tournaments. As anyone who has played it can understand, Halve-It is sometimes known as Murder.

NUMBER OF PLAYERS:
Any number can play.

NUMBERS IN PLAY:
20, 16, double 7, 14, triple 10, 17, double bull's-eye.

RULES OF THE GAME:
Players take turns throwing at the numbers in play, in

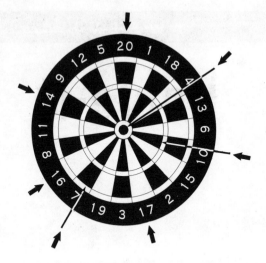

the sequence as listed above, beginning with 20 and ending with double bull's-eye, scoring as many points as possible. Only the darts hitting the specific number in play count. If a player misses a number entirely in a turn, his or her cumulative score is cut in half; hence the name of the game. For instance, if a player has a cumulative score of 76 after two turns (having scored three 20s on the first turn and one 16 on the second) and then misses the next number—double 7—with all three darts, the player's score is cut in half, leaving 38. If the first number, 20, is missed entirely, the score remains at zero. If an odd-numbered score is halved, the score is rounded up (for example, 51 halved would be 26).

The player with the most points at the end of the game wins. In the rare case of a tie, players may opt to replay the double bull's-eye or another number, or the person with the least number of halved scores in the game may be declared the winner.

STRATEGIES FOR SUCCESSFUL PLAY:

Given the range of numbers, including doubles and triples, accuracy is critical in Halve-It, and a player who is good at triples and accurate on the double bull's-eye is likely to win often. Since the double bull's-eye is last and is usually the most difficult number to hit, many scores are cut in half on the last turn.

SCORING:

The scoreboard for Halve-It is a basic scoring grid with players' initials on top and the target numbers noted vertically on the left. The cumulative score is noted after each turn.

	SAMPLE GAME	
	A	B
20	40	60
16	(16)	(32)
	56	92
D7	(0)	(14)
	28*	106
14	(56)	(42)
	84	148
T10	(30)	(0)
	114	74*
17	(68)	(51)
	182	126
DB	(0)	(50)
	91*	176

Halve-It scoreboard at the end of a game.
Turn scores in parenthesies; * denotes halved scores.

Variations:

➤ *Halve-It With Cricket Numbers.* All the rules of Halve-It apply in this variation, which uses the numbers used in Cricket—20, 19, 18, 17, 16, 15, and bull's-eye. This game is particularly good practice for regular Cricket players.

➤ *Halve-It With Triples and Doubles.* This is a somewhat easier variation of the standard game, subject to the same Halve-It rules. The numbers in play are 12, 13, 14, triple (any triple must be hit or the score is halved), 15, 16, 17, double (any double must be hit or the score is halved), 18, 19, and single bull's-eye.

➤ *Halve-It, Random Numbers.* Halve-It may be played with any selection of target numbers, and some play it with numbers picked at random (possibly including specific doubles and triples).

➤ *Halve-It, Beginning Negative.* Sometimes Halve-It is played with the rule that if the first number is missed, a negative score is given (instead of remaining at zero). For instance, if 20, the first number, is missed, then −20 is scored.

Scram

S cram is a game of accuracy covering all the numbers on the dartboard, without the bull's-eye. It's an exciting, highly competitive game played in two separate rounds of play.

NUMBER OF PLAYERS:
Two players or two teams.

NUMBERS IN PLAY:
All the numbers, 1 through 20, are used.

Rules of the Game:

At the beginning of the game, after determining the order of play, one player becomes the "scorer" and the other is the "stopper." Generally, the stopper throws first. The task for the scorer is to score as many points as possible by hitting any of the numbers on the board. The stopper's task is to hit each number, 1-20, once, in any part of the number, in any order. As each number is hit, it is erased or crossed out on the scoreboard, and the scorer can no longer score points on that number.

Scoring stops when all the numbers are erased. Then the scorer notes his or her final score on the scoreboard and the scoring and stopping roles are reversed. The game is played in two separate rounds, with each player throwing an entire round as both stopper and scorer. The winner is the player who scores the most points as scorer.

Strategies for Successful Play:

Accuracy, especially on the high numbers early in the game, is the key to Scram for both scorer and stopper. The scorer wants the highest numbers for score, and the stopper wants to erase these numbers from the board as quickly as possible.

Any number that has not been erased from the scoreboard can be hit for points. For example, if the scorer is aiming at 20s on his first turn and hits 1, 5, and 20, they all may count for score if none has been erased. The same holds true for the stopper, and an opening turn with the same results, hitting 1, 5, and 20, would allow him or her to erase these three numbers.

A		B
20	X	40
19	X	(70)
18	X	110
17	X	
16	X	
15		
14		
13		
12		
11		
10		
9		
8		
7		
6		
5	X	
4		
3		
2		
1		

Scram scoreboard after two turns X denotes
numbers erased by stopper. Scorer's cumulative
score noted, with turn score in parenthesis.

SCORING:

The scoreboard is a simple vertical list of the numbers
20–1, in descending order, with players' initials at the

top. The stopper erases or crosses out the numbers as they are hit. The scorer keeps his or her cumulative score adjacent to the numbers.

Sample Game:

First turn

Player A, stopper, hits 5, 20, and 19 and crosses them out.

Player B, scorer, hits two 18s and a 4. Score: 40.

Second turn

Player A, stopper, hits 18, 17, 16 and crosses them out.

Player B, scorer, hits triple 15, 15, 10. Score: 70.

Play continues until all the numbers are hit by the stopper and erased; the stopper and scorer roles are then reversed.

FOURTEEN

English Cricket

English Cricket, not to be be confused with American Cricket (see Chapter 4), is a challenging British game that takes its form and terminology—bowler, batter, and wicket—from the field game of the same name and is played in two separate rounds of play. Some call it Bowlers And Batters.

Number of Players:
Two players or two teams.

NUMBERS IN PLAY:

All the numbers are used, but since each score must exceed 40, the high numbers—especially 20—are the favorites.

RULES OF THE GAME:

One player becomes the batter, and the other is the bowler; the batter goes first. Ten stripes are entered on the board as wickets. The bowler's task is to erase these wickets by hitting bull's-eyes: With each single bull's-eye, one wicket is erased, and with each double bull's-eye, two wickets are erased. The batter's task is to score as many points or runs while any wickets remain, but only scores over 40 count. For example, a score of 38 would score no runs, a score of 41 would score one run, a score of 60 would score 20, and so on.

Scoring stops when all 10 wickets are erased (or crossed out) by the bowler. The batter notes his or her final score on the scoreboard, and the roles are reversed. The game is played in two separate rounds, with each player throwing an entire round as batter and bowler. The winner is the player with the most points, or runs, from his or her round as batter.

STRATEGIES FOR SUCCESSFUL PLAY:

Accuracy, not strategy, is the key to English Cricket. Some players may prefer being either the bowler or the batter first.

SCORING:

The scoreboard has 10 stripes, denoting wickets, for the bowler, and a space for scoring for the batter.

SAMPLE GAME:

First turn:

Player A, batter, hits 20, 20, and double 20. Total score: 80; English Cricket score (since only scores over 40 count): 40.

Player B, bowler, hits one bull's-eye and erases one wicket.

Second turn:

Player A, batter, hits 20, 1, and 5. Total score: 26; English Cricket score (since it's under 40): 0

Player B, bowler, hits one double bull's-eye and one single bull's-eye and erases three wickets.

Bowler	Batter
/ /	40
/ /	
/ /	

English Cricket scoreboard after two turns. The bowler has erased four wickets; the batter has 40 points.

FIFTEEN

Other Games and Practice Routines

The best practice for anyone, at any skill level, is to play regularly against good competition and with helpful, knowledgeable partners. But when a match isn't available, one can play any of the games in this book alone or invent practice routines based on individual strengths and weaknesses.

Although there is no right or wrong way to practice, practice time should be spent on fundamental skills and on the target numbers that relate to favorite games. The physical mechanics of the game should also be given serious attention: This is the time to experiment with grip or stance or throwing techniques and to work on basic skills. Similarly, practice should always include honing your concentration; developing a solid mental focus in practice can greatly increase the chances of winning in competition.

When practicing a particular game, keep track of the number of darts thrown. For instance, an exceptional Cricket or 301 game would take only five or six turns—15 to 18 darts. An above-average game would take seven to nine turns—21 to 27 darts. Ending either game in under 30 darts (10 turns) is a realistic goal to shoot for.

Also, when practicing a specific game, the best players often keep track of the number of turns, keep score, and tabulate a points-per-dart (PPD) and points-per-turn (PPT) average and try to better their individual statistics with each practice session.

Good Practice Games

➤ Fifty-One, Fifty-Seven, and Other Variations ◄

Fifty-One is a particularly good game for practicing some of the numbers used in Cricket. The object of the game is to make a score of exactly 51 in each turn, with one dart (by hitting the triple 17) or with all three, using all the numbers on the board as necessary (a triple 17 or three single 17s are best, however). Players keep track of how many times each hits 51.

A common variation of Fifty-One is Fifty-Seven, in which the number 19 is played (triple 19 is 57). Similarly, to practice 18s, you could play Fifty-Four.

➤ Best of Ten ◄

A good warm-up, either alone or against an opponent, is to keep track of the best of 10 darts at a given number. The number chosen is usually one used in popular games, such as 20, 19, or bull's-eye, as practice for Cricket or '01. But aiming for a number that is seldom played, such as 7, 3, or 6, is also good practice for general accuracy. Or you could take 10 turns (30 darts) at an individual number and keep track of the number of times the number is hit.

➤ Call Three ◄

A good practice routine for accuracy and for learning the dartboard is to pick three numbers at random before each turn and attempt them, in order. This practice routine can also be made into a game with two or more players, with one player calling out three numbers for the other. For example, 3, 6, and 20 are called; these numbers are then attempted, and a score of 1, 2, or 3 is noted, depending on how many of the numbers are hit. This is good practice for changing numbers in the middle of a turn, which is particularly useful in Cricket and '01.

➤ Round the World and Its Variations ◄

Just like the games played by two or more players, Round the World, Round the World—Doubles, and Round the World—Triples are great practice routines that are used by top players and beginners alike (see Chapter 11).

➤ Doubles Practice ◄

Playing an entire game of Round the World—Doubles might be too ambitious for many, but skill in hitting the doubles that are most commonly used in '01 is necessary for success in that game. These numbers are 20, 16, 12, 8, 4, 2, and 1. Hitting the doubles of these seven numbers in seven turns (one per every three-dart turn) would be a good beginning goal to strive for.

➤ Sixty Or More ◄

In games requiring high scores, particularly the '01 games, it is important to be accurate on the 20—the highest and, hence, most popular number on the dartboard. For practice on the 20, either alone or against an opponent, players take 10 turns at the 20 and keep track of how many times a score of 60 or more is achieved. Five out of 10 is good, seven out of 10 very good, and eight or more is excellent.

The same routine could be used on the 19, 18, or any other practice number, with the triple score being the optimum score per turn (e.g., 57 for 19, 54 for 18). Another good game for scoring practice is Legs (see Chapter 9).

➤ Bull's-eye Practice ◄

Even if one plays games in which the bull's-eye is seldom used ('01, for example), the bull's-eye is important and should be practiced regularly. Even in games in which the bull's-eye is not used, the standard convention for choosing the game and the order of play is shooting for cork, and the player closest to the bull's-eye begins the game. In virtually all games, and particularly in Cricket and '01, throwing first is a considerable advantage and is often the deciding factor in close games. It is not surprising, then, that all good players practice throwing at the bull's-eye, and that their pregame warm-up darts always include a few darts at it, even if only in preparation for shooting for cork.

Publications

Double Eagle Newsletter
American Darts Organization
652 S. Brookhurst Ave. #543
Anaheim, CA 92804
Phone: (714) 254-0212
Fax: (714) 254-0214
Published by the American Darts Organization four times a year and supplied to all ADO members ($20 annual membership fee; $16 annual renewal). Includes news and articles on the regional, national, and international activities of the American Darts Organization and its members.

Bull's-Eye News
281 E. Broadway
Westerville, OH 43081
(614) 899-1338; toll-free (800) 688-DART (3278)
Fax: (614) 899-6696
Published monthly; covers the national and international darts scene, with special attention to U.S. tournament news and results, with a variety of dart-related articles and player profiles. Annual subscription, 12 issues: $24 (24 issues: $44; 36 issues: $60; six-month trial subscription: $14).

Darts World
9 Kelsey Park Road
Beckenham, Kent BR3 2LH
England
Phone (from U.S.): 011-44-81-650-6580
Fax (from U.S.): 011-44-81-650-2534
Published monthly in England; covers the international darts scene, and highlights the darts news, personalities, and the many tournaments of the United Kingdom. Annual subscription: $36.

Throw Lines Magazine
National Dart Association
6620 River Parkway
Wauwatosa, WI 53213
(414) 476-4665
Fax: (414) 476-8181
Published quarterly; the official National Dart Association publication, devoted entirely to the sport of electronic darts, with news, articles, and tournament schedules and results. Annual subscription: $15.

Where to Play Darts and Where to Buy Darts

People often get interested in darts from playing with friends at a tavern or restaurant. Others learn at home and then start looking for a league to join. To locate local leagues, inquire at dart-supply houses, any tavern that has a dartboard (notices of league games are often posted near the board, complete with names and addresses of league managers), or a local sporting-goods store. Usually a few inquiries will yield results, and many larger leagues have their own publications.

With the growing popularity of darts, most sporting-goods stores are now stocking darts, dartboards, and accessories. Also, the number of retailers that deal only in darts and dart supplies is growing rapidly. In fact, in major cities, there is often a heading in the Yellow Pages under Darts. There are also a number of mail-order retailers. If you are unable to find dart supplies or want detailed information on mail-order suppliers, consult the advertising pages of dart publications (see Appendix A).

Recommended Two-and Three-Dart Finishes For '01 Games: Out Chart

An Out Chart is included here for easy reference. Beginning players may want to photocopy or enlarge this chart and post it near the dartboard. For a complete explanation of how to read this chart, and the logic behind its recommendations, see Chapter 5.

T = Triple; D = Double; S = Single; B = Bull's-eye

170 - T20, T20, DB.	127 - T20, T17, D8.	91 - T17, D20.	55 - S15, D20.
167 - T20, T19, DB.	126 - T19, T15, D12.	90 - T18, D18.	54 - S14, D20.
164 - T20, T18, DB.	125 - T18, T13, D16.	89 - T19, D16.	53 - S13, D20.
161 - T20, T17, DB	124 - T20, T16, D8.	88 - T16, D20.	52 - S12, D20.
160 - T20, T20, D20.	123 - T19, T14, D12.	87 - T17, D18.	51 - S11, D20.
158 - T20, T20, D19.	122 - T18, T20, D4.	86 - T18, D16.	50 - S10, D20.
157 - T20, T19, D20.	121 - T17, T18, D8.	85 - T15, D20.	49 - S9, D20.
156 - T20, T20, D18.	120 - T20, S20, D20.	84 - T20, D12.	48 - S8, D20.
155 - T20, T19, D19.	119 - T19, T10, D16.	83 - T17, D16.	47 - S15, D16.
154 - T20, T18, D20.	118 - T20, S18, D20.	82 - T14, D20.	46 - S14, D16.
153 - T20, T19, D18.	117 - T20, S17, D20.	81 - T19, D12.	45 - S13, D16.
152 - T20, T20, D16.	116 - T20, S16, D20.	80 - T20, D10.	44 - S12, D16.
151 - T20, T17, D20.	115 - T19, S18, D20.	79 - T13, D20.	43 - S11, D16.
150 - T20, T18, D18.	114 - T20, S14, D20.	78 - T18, D12.	42 - S10, D16.
149 - T20, T19, D16.	113 - T19, S16, D20.	77 - T15, D16.	41 - S9, D16.
148 - T20, T16, D20.	112 - T20, S12, D20.	76 - T20, D8.	39 - S7, D16.
147 - T20, T17, D18.	111 - T19, S14, D20.	75 - T17, D12.	37 - S5, D16.
146 - T20, T18, D16.	110 - T20, S10, D20.	74 - T14, D16.	35 - S3, D16.
145 - T20, T15, D20.	109 - T20, S9, D20.	73 - T19, D8.	33 - S1, D16.
144 - T20, T20, D12.	108 - T19, S19, D16.	72 - T16, D12.	31 - S7, D12.
143 - T19, T18, D16.	107 - T20, S15, D16.	71 - T13, D16.	29 - S13, D8.
142 - T19, T14, D20.	106 - T20, S14, D16.	70 - T18, D8.	27 - S11, D8.
141 - T20, T19, D12.	105 - T19, S8, D20.	69 - T15, D12.	25 - S9, D8.
140 - T20, T20, D10.	104 - T18, S10, D20.	68 - T20, D4.	23 - S7, D8.
139 - T19, T14, D20.	103 - T17, S12, D20.	67 - T17, D8.	21 - S5, D8.
138 - T20, T18, D12.	102 - T19, S13, D16.	66 - T14, D12.	19 - S3, D8.
137 - T17, T18, D16.	101 - T17, S10, D20.	65 - T11, D16.	17 - S13, D2.
136 - T20, T20, D8.	100 - T20, D20.	64 - T16, D8.	15 - S7, D4.
135 - T20, T17, D12.	99 - T19, S10, D16.	63 - T13, D12.	13 - S5, D4.
134 - T20, T14, D16.	98 - T20, D19.	62 - T10, D16.	11 - S3, D4.
133 - T20, T19, D8.	97 - T19, D20.	61 - T15, D8.	9 - S1, D4.
132 - T20, T16, D12.	96 - T20, D18.	60 - S20, D20.	7 - S3, D2.
131 - T20, T13, D16.	95 - T19, D19.	59 - S19, D20.	5 - S1, D2.
130 - T20, T18, D8.	94 - T18, D20.	58 - S18, D20.	3 - S1, D1.
129 - T19, T16, D12.	93 - T19, D18.	57 - S17, D20.	
128 - T18, T14, D16.	92 - T20, D16.	56 - S16, D20.	

American Darts Organization Tournament Rules

American Darts Organization

TOURNAMENT RULES

GLOSSARY OF TERMS

The following terms/meanings shall apply when used in the body of these Tournament Rules.

ADO: American Darts Organization

Match: The total number of Legs being competed for between two players/teams

Leg/Game: That element of a Match recognized as a fixed odd number. i.e., 301/501/1001

Scorer: Scorekeeper, Marker or Chalker

Cork: Bullseye or Bull

Masculine: Masculine gender nouns or pronouns shall include female

Singular: Singular terms shall, where necessary, include the plural

PLAYING RULES

All darts events played under the exclusive supervision of and/or sanctioned by the ADO, shall be played in accordance with the following rules.

GENERAL

1. All players/teams shall play by these Tournament Rules and, where necessary, any supplemental Rules stipulated by local Tournament Organizers.

2. Any player/team who, during the course of any event, fails to comply with any of these Tournament Rules, shall be subject to disqualification from that event.

3. The interpretation of these Tournament Rules, in relation to a specific darts event, shall rest with the local Tournament Organizers, whose decisions shall be final and binding. Protests after the fact shall not be considered.

4. Good sportsmanship shall be the prevailing attitude throughout the tournament.

5. Gambling is neither permitted nor sanctioned by the ADO.

6. The ADO will, in the course of Tournament Sanctioning, ensure, to the best of its ability, that the host/sponsor organization for a darts event has the funding and/or sponsorship necessary to support the advertised cash prize structure for same. The manner and matter of tournament prize payments shall be the responsibility of the respective host/sponsor organization and not that of the ADO.

7. The ADO assumes no responsibility for accident or injury on the premises.

8. The ADO reserves the right to add to or amend, any, or all, of the ADO Tournament Rules, at any time for any purpose deemed necessary at that time.

PROCEDURAL

9. Decisions regarding the prize structure and event schedule, the method of player registration, and the choice of the match pairing system, shall be left at the discretion of the local Tournament Organizers.

10. Nine darts warm-up is the maximum allowance per player.

11. Tournament boards are reserved for assigned match pairings only. Boards are not to be used for practice, unless so designated by the Tournament Organizers.

12. Match pairings will be called 3 times only (minimum of 5 minutes between calls). Should a player/team fail to report to the assigned board within the 15 minute allotted time, a Forfeit will be called. **NOTE:** Should a player/team be called to matches in two concurrent events (e.g. a female playing in both a Ladies' Only and an Open event), that player/team must choose in which event he/they wish to continue play. A Forfeit will be called, unless that player/team can reach their assigned board within the regulation (15 minute) time period described above.

13. Should a player's playing equipment become damaged, or be lost during the course of a throw, that player shall be allowed up to a maximum of 5 minutes in which to repair/replace the playing equipment.

14. A maximum time limit of 5 minutes, under exceptional circumstances subject to the permission of a Tournament Official, shall be allowed in the instance of a player requiring to leave the playing area, during the course of matchplay.

15. Players and Scorers ONLY are allowed inside the playing area.

16. Opposing players must stand at least 2 feet behind the player at the Hockey.

THROW

17. All darts must be thrown by, and from, the hand.

18. A Throw shall consist of three darts, unless a Leg/Match is completed in a lesser amount.

19. Should a player 'touch' any dart, which is in the dartboard, during a throw, that throw shall be deemed to have been completed.

20. Any dart bouncing off, or falling out of the dartboard, shall not be rethrown.

STARTING AND FINISHING   **(ALL EVENTS)**

21. All Matches will be begun by THROWING THE CORK. The
     player throwing the Cork 1st will be decided by a coin flip,
     with the winner having the option of throwing 1st or 2nd.
     The player throwing closest to the Cork shall throw first in
     the 1st Leg. The Loser of the 1st Leg has the option of
     throwing the Cork first in the 2nd Leg. If a 3rd Leg is
     necessary, the Cork will again be thrown, with the loser of
     the original coin flip having the option of throwing first for
     the Cork.

22. The second thrower may acknowledge the first dart as
     an inner or outer Bull (Cork) and ask for that dart to be
     removed prior to his throw. Should the first dart be removed
     without the request of the 2nd thrower, a rethrow will occur;
     with the 2nd thrower now having the option of throwing
     first. The dart must remain in the board in order to count.
     Additional throws may be made when throwing the Cork,
     until such time as the player's dart remains in the board.
     Should the 2nd thrower dislodge the dart of the 1st, a
     rethrow will be made with the 2nd thrower now throwing
     first. Rethrows shall be called if the scorer cannot decide
     which dart is closet to the Cork, or if both darts are
     anywhere in the inner bull, or both darts are anywhere in
     the outer bull. Decision of the scorer is final. Should
     a rethrow be necessary, the darts will be removed and
     the person who threw 2nd will now throw 1st.

23. In all events, each Leg shall be played with a Straight Start
     (no double required), and a double will be required to
     finish, unless otherwise stated by the local Tournament
     Organizers.

24. For the purpose of starting and finishing a Leg/Match, the
     INNER BULL is considered a double 25.

25. The 'BUST RULE' shall apply. (If the player scores one less,
     equal, or more points than needed to reach zero, he has
     "busted". His score reverts back to the score required prior
     to the beginning of his throw.)

26. Fast finishes such as 3 in a bed, 222, 111, shanghai, etc., do
     not apply.

27. A Leg/Match is concluded at such time as a player/team
     hits the 'double' required to reduce their remaining score to
     zero. Any and all darts thrown subsequently, shall not
     count for score.

(DOUBLES / TEAM EVENTS)

28. It is permissible for the Doubles/Team player finishing a
     Leg, to throw the Cork and start the subsequent Leg. It is
     also permissible for one member of a Doubles or Team to

throw the Cork 1st, and have his partner or teammate shoot first.

29. It is permissible for a Doubles or Team to participate with fewer than the required number of players, provided that team forfeits a turn(s) in each rotation, equal to the number of missing players. The missing player(s) may NOT join a Leg in progress, but is allowed to participate in a subsequent Leg(s) of that Match.

30. No player may participate on more than one Doubles or Team, in any respective darts event. There shall be NO recycling of players (either male or female) under any circumstances.

31. No substitutes shall be allowed after the first round of Doubles/Team play.

SCORING

32. For a dart to score, it must remain in the board 5 seconds after the 3rd or final dart has been thrown by that player. The tip of the dart point must be touching the bristle portion of the board, in order for that dart to be counted as score.

33. No dart may be touched by the thrower, another player, scorer, or spectator, prior to the decision of the scorer. Should this occur, that throw shall be deemed to have been completed, per provisions set forth in Rule 19.

34. A dart's score shall be determined from the side of the wire at which the point of the dart enters the board. Should a dart lodge directly between the connecting wires on the dartboard, making it impossible to determine on which side of the wire the dart resides, the score shall always be the higher value of the two segments in question. This includes the outside double ring for the game shot. Determination as to whether the dart is directly between the wires shall be made in accordance with Rule 33.

35. It is the responsibility of the player to verify his score before removing his darts from the board. The score remains as written if one or more darts has been removed from the board. Errors in arithmetic must stand as written, unless corrected prior to the beginning of that player's next throw. In case of Doubles/Team matches, such errors must be rectified prior to the next turn of any partner/player on that team.

36. In Doubles/Team events, no player may throw (during a Leg) until each of his teammates has completed his throw. The FIRST player throwing out of turn shall receive a score of ZERO points for that round and his Team shall FORFEIT such turn.

37. The Scorer shall mark the board so that scores made are listed in the outer columns of the scoreboard, and the totals remaining are listed in the two middle columns.

38. The scoreboard/sheet must be clearly visible in front of the player at the Hockey.

39. The Scorer may inform the thrower what he has scored and/or what he has left. He MAY NOT inform the thrower what he has left in terms of number combinations. It IS permissible for a partner, teammate, or a spectator to advise the thrower during the course of a Match.

EQUIPMENT   (DARTS)

40. Darts used in tournament play shall not exceed an overall maximum length of 30.5 cm (12 in.), nor weigh more than 50 gm per dart. Each dart shall consist of a recognizable point, barrel, and flight.

(DARTBOARD)

41. The dartboard shall be a standard 18" bristle board, of the type approved by the ADO (Sportcraft/Nodor), and shall be of the standard 1 - 20 clock pattern.

INTERNATIONAL DARTBOARD

Double Score
Twice the number)

Single Score
(Face Value)

Triple Score
(Triple the number)

Inner Bull
Double 25
or (50 points)

Outer Bull
(25 points)

Out of Play Area
(No score)

STANDARD DIMENSIONS

Double and Triple rings inside width measurement	= 8 mm. (5/16 ins)
Inner Bull inside diameter	= 12.7 mm. (0.5 ins)
Outer Bull inside diameter	= 31 mm. (1.25 ins)
Outside edge of Double wire to Center Bull	= 170 mm. (6.75 ins)
Outside edge of Triple wire to Center Bull	= 117 mm. (4.25 ins)
Outside edge of Double wire to Outside edge of Double wire	= 342 mm. (13.5 ins)
Overall dartboard diameter	= 457 mm. (18.0 ins)
Spider wire gauge (Maximum Standard Wire Gauge)	= 16 SWG.

42. The scoring wedge indicated by 20 shall be the darker of the two wedge colors and must be the top center wedge.

43. No alterations/accessories may be added to the board setups.

44. The inner narrow band shall score 'Triple' the segment number and the outer narrow band shall score 'Double' the segment number.

45. The outer center ring shall score '25' and inner center ring shall score '50' and shall be called the 'Bull'.

46. The minimum throwing distance shall be 7'9¼". The board height shall be 5'8" (floor to center bull; 9'7½" measured diagonally from the center bull to the back of the raised hockey at floor level).

(LIGHTING)

47. Lights must be affixed in such a way as to brightly illuminate the board, reduce to a minimum the shadows cast by the darts, and not physically impedge the flight of a dart.

(HOCKEY)

48. Whenever possible, a raised hockey, at least 1½" high and 2' long, shall be placed in position at the minimum throwing distance, and shall measure from the back of the raised hockey 7'9¼" along the floor to a plumb line at the face of the dartboard.

49. In the event the hockey is a tape or similar 'flush' marking, the minimum throwing distance shall be measured from the edge (front) of the tape closest to the dartboard.

OTHER DIMENSIONS

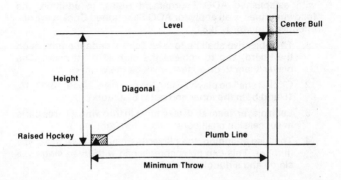

50. Should a player have any portion of his feet or shoes over the hockey line during a throw, all darts so thrown shall be counted as part of his throw, but any score made by said darts shall be invalid and not counted. One warning by the official shall be considered sufficient before invoking this rule.

51. A player wishing to throw a dart, or darts, from a point either side of the hockey line, must keep his feet behind an imaginary straight line extending from either side of the hockey line.

Center Bull Height	= 1.73 **metres** (5 ft · 8 ins)
Minimum Throwing Distance	= 2.37 metres (7 ft · 9 ¼ ins)
Diagonal · Center Bull to back of Hockey	= 2.93 metres (9 ft · 7 ½ ins)
Height of raised Hockey	= 38 mm. (1 ½ ins)
Length of raised Hockey	= 610 mm. (2 ft · 0 ins)
Conversion factor	= 1 cm. (0.3937 ins)

$$\text{Diagonal length} = \sqrt{\text{Height}^2 + \text{Hockey}^2}$$

$$= \sqrt{1.73^2 + 2.37^2}$$

$$= \sqrt{2.9929 + 5.6169}$$

$$= \sqrt{8.6098}$$

$$= 2.934 \text{ metres (9 ft · 7 ½ ins)}$$

(SCOREBOARD)

52. A scoreboard must be mounted within 4' laterally from the dartboard and at not more than a 45 degree angle from the dartboard.

Approved August 21, 1981

ADO AMERICAN CRICKET RULES

All darts events played under the exclusive supervision of and/or sanctioned by the ADO, shall be played in accordance with established ADO Tournament Rules. In addition, the following rules shall apply for ADO Sanctioned Cricket events, effective January 1, 1984.

1. The objective shall be to 'own'/'close' certain numbers on the board, and to achieve the highest point score. The player/team to do so first, shall be the winner.

2. Cricket shall be played using the numbers 20, 19, 18, 17, 16, 15 and both the inner and outer bull (cork).

3. Each player/team shall take turns in throwing. (Three darts in succession shall constitute a 'turn'/'inning'.)

4. To close an inning, the player/team must score three of a number. This can be accomplished with three singles, a single and a double, or a triple.

5. Once a player/team scores three of a number, it is 'owned' by that player/team. Once both players/teams have scored three of a number, it is 'closed', and no further scoring can be accomplished on that number by either player/team.

6. To close the bullseye, the outer bull counts as a single, and the inner bull counts as a double.

7. Once a player/team closes an inning, he/they may score points on that number until the opponent also closes that inning. All numerical scores shall be added to the previous balance.

8. Numbers can be 'owned' or 'closed' in any order desired by the individual player/team. Calling your shot is not required.

9. For the purpose of 'owning' a number, the double and triple ring shall count as 2 or 3, respectively. Three marks will close an inning.

10. After a number is 'owned' by a team, the double and triple ring shall count as 2 or 3 times the numerical values, respectively.

11. Winning the game:
    a. The player/team that closes all innings first and has the most points, shall be declared the winner.
    b. If both sides are tied on points, or have no points, the first player/team to close all innings shall be the winner.
    c. If a player/team closes all innings first, and is behind in points, he/they must continue to score on any innings not closed until either the point deficit is made up, or the opponent has closed all innings.

12. It shall be the responsibility of the player to verify his score before removing his darts from the board. The score remains as written if one or more darts has been removed from the board. In accordance with the inherent "strategy" involved in the Cricket game, no alterations in score shall be allowed, after the fact.

AMERICAN DARTS ORGANIZATION
APPROVED 8/19/83
REVISED 8/14/86
REVISED 11/14/87
REVISED 1/1/89
REVISED 3/10/91

ADO INDIVIDUAL MEMBERSHIP APPLICATION

The American Darts Organization (ADO) is the official national darts organization, as recognized by the World Darts Federation. Membership in the ADO is limited to U.S. residents only.

An ADO Individual Membership entitles the member to:

— a copy of the ADO Tournament Calendar, listing major darting events throughout the U.S. during the current calendar year.

— a 1-year subscription to "Double Eagle" newsletter, the official quarterly publication of the ADO.

— a wallet-size ADO membership card, bearing the member's name.

— a 3-color metal ADO Pin *

— a 3-color cloth ADO Patch *

— a copy of the ADO Rules Book *

— a copy of the ADO Handbook *

— a quarterly Individual Report of the member's ADO Championship Points

If you are interested in becoming a member of the American Darts Organization, please complete the following tear-off application. Send it, with payment to: ADO, 7621 E. Firestone Bl. Ste. E6, Downey, CA 90241

TEAR OFF

I hereby apply for Individual Membership in the American Darts Organization.

NAME _____

ADDRESS _____

CITY _____ STATE _____ ZIP _____

I include a check/money order made payable to the ADO for the following:

- ❏ Annual Membership $20.00   (includes all items listed above)
- ❏ Renewal $16.00   (* items not included)
- ❏ Additional ADO Cloth Patch $ 3.00   (includes shipping costs)

NOTE: ADO memberships are renewable annually.

Mail this tear-off form, together with a check/money order for the amount(s) indicated above to:

AMERICAN DARTS ORGANIZATION
652 S. Brookhurst Ave. #543
Anaheim, CA 92804
Phone: (714) 254-0212
Fax: (714) 254-0214

For Office
Use
Only   Date: _____   ADO Region: _____

Glossary of Common Dart Terms

ARROWS. Slang for darts.

BARREL. The metal body of the dart where it is gripped.

BED. A section of a number; usually used when referring to triples and doubles (e.g., the triple 20 bed). All three darts in the same triple is called Three in a Bed.

BED AND BREAKFAST. A British term for the score of 26 in an '01 game, from hitting a 20 and one each of the adjacent numbers, 1 and 5.

BOTTOM OF THE BOARD. The numbers on the bottom half of the dartboard.

BULL. The bull's-eye, which has an Outer Bull and an Inner Bull.

BUSTED. Too many points scored.

CORK. The bull's-eye.

DIDDLE FOR THE MIDDLE. Slang for the game-beginning convention of shooting for the cork, in which the player who throws a dart closest to the bull's-eye goes first.

DIRTY DARTS. Derogatory slang for questionable tactics (e.g., excessive point scoring in a game, far beyond what would be necessary to win).

DOUBLE BULL or DOUBLE CORK. The smaller, center portion of the bull's-eye, also known as the Inner Bull.

DOUBLE-IN. Hitting the double area of a number to begin a game.

DOUBLE-OUT. Hitting the double area of a number to end a game.

DOUBLE TOP. The double 20.

EIGHTS. Slang for 18s in Cricket.

FALLOUT. Slang for unintended, but scorable, darts (e.g., hitting an 18 when aiming for the 20, but being able to score the 18).

FAT. The largest part of the number. To shoot "fat" is to aim for a sure and safe single.

FIVES. Slang for 15s in Cricket.

FLIGHT. The "feathers" of the dart that give it aerodynamic float.

GOOD GROUP! A compliment for tight, accurate throwing.

HOCKEY. A raised 1½-inch board used to mark the throwing line.

INNING. A round of completed turns by both players, or a turn in a particular game that has innings, like Baseball or Shanghai.

LEG. A game in a match, as "the best of five legs," in which each leg is an entire game. Or, in the game of Legs, a stripe on the board.

MATCH. A series of complete games (legs). Matches are usually the best of three or five games.

MUGS AWAY. Slang term for a convention whereby the loser of a game may start the next game immediately (without shooting for cork).

NINES. Slang for 19 in Cricket.

OCHE. Alternate spelling of Hockey (pronounced "ockey").

PIE. Any of the numbered segments on the dartboard.

POINT MONGERING or **POINT FREAKING.** Derogatory term for shooting excessive points, usually in the game of Cricket.

RIGHT THERE! Encouraging words for a just-missed dart.

ROBIN HOOD. Whenever a dart strikes and sticks into another dart on the dartboard, named after the famous archer.

ROUND. Any three-dart turn.

ROUND OF NINE. A perfect turn in most games in which three triples are scored (e.g., in Cricket, an opening round of nine could be T20, T19, and T18). Similarly, all turns can be tabulated as a "round of . . ." (in which the total quantity of the round or three-dart turn is tabulated by including all the singles, doubles, and triples).

SET. Any three-dart turn. In some places a score of 60 in '01 games—usually three single 20s—is called a set, and is scored as an S.

SEVENS. Slang for 17s in Cricket.

SHAFT. The middle section of the dart that holds the Flight.

SHANGHAI. Hitting a triple, double, and a single of the same number in a three-dart turn; also the game of the same name.

SHOOTING FOR CORK or **SHOOTING FOR BULL.** The usual game-beginning convention whereby each player, or a player from each team, throws one dart at the bull's-eye to determine the game to be played and who goes first.

SIXES. Slang for 16s in Cricket.

TON. A score of 100 points, scored as a T.

TON-EIGHTY. A score of 180, the highest score possible on the dartboard (three triple 20s), scored as T80.

TON-FORTY. A score of 140, scored as T40.

TON-TWENTY. A score of 120, scored as T20.

TOP OF THE BOARD. The numbers on the top half of the dartboard.

TOPS. The double 20, also known as Double Top.

TOUGH DARTS. A common saying when darts *almost* hit their mark.

WEDGE. A section or sections of the dartboard.